Better Homes and Gardens®

LOW-FAT MEALS

Our seal assures you that every recipe
in *Low-Fat Meals*
has been tested in the Better Homes
and Gardens® Test Kitchen. This means
that each recipe is practical and
reliable, and meets our high standards
of taste appeal.

© Copyright 1990 by Meredith Corporation, Des Moines, Iowa. All Rights Reserved. Printed in the United States of America. First Edition. First Printing.

Library of Congress Catalog Card Number: 89-63154 ISBN: 0-696-01889-6

Like many people, I always intended to start my low-fat diet tomorrow. I knew that reducing fat would be a step toward better health. But, I love to eat and hated the thought of giving up my favorite foods.

Once I started my work on *Low-Fat Meals,* however, I discovered I could reduce fat and still enjoy great-tasting foods. I was able to develop many new recipes using naturally low-fat foods. For instance, I discovered that one of the lean fresh turkey cuts is the perfect meat for sweet-and-sour *Turkey Kabobs*. And, I was even able to cut the fat in many of my favorite recipes, such as *Swiss Steak, Chicken Parmigiano,* and *Chocolate Sauce.*

With the aid of these scrumptiously healthy recipes, I now choose low-fat foods. You can, too. Look through these pages to see all the delicious dishes you can enjoy on your low-fat diet.

Mary Major

Editor
Low-Fat Meals

Pasta Salad
(see recipe, page 96)

Yogurt-Topped Fruit
(see recipe, page 112)

On the front cover: Poached Salmon Steaks (see recipe, page 65), Lemon Pasta (see recipe, page 83), Fruit Compote (see recipe, page 106)

Fish Creole
(see recipe, page 62)

Contents

❧

Cooking the Low-Fat Way

Questions & Answers

You want to reduce the fat in your diet, but you're afraid it's easier said than done. Help is here! This section provides answers to some commonly asked questions about the foods to buy and how to cook them.

Smart Food Choices

What's my best choice in the meat aisle for my low-fat diet?
Fish, poultry, and meat all fit into your new diet. Lean fish is the best choice because it contains the least amount of saturated fat. Poultry is also an excellent choice, and is even lower in fat if you remove the skin. Beef, pork, and other meats are acceptable as long as you choose lean cuts and trim off and discard visible fat.

How big a serving of meat can I eat?
Limit your serving size to 3 ounces. Because meat, fish, and poultry all contain saturated fat and cholesterol, eat only two servings a day.

What kinds of red meat are lean enough for my low-fat diet?
Beef cuts from the round, sirloin, chuck, and loin are usually lean. All cuts of veal are

acceptable. For pork, choose cuts from the loin and the leg, and for lamb, cuts from the leg, arm, and loin.

Avoid organ meats, like liver, since they are very high in cholesterol. Also, avoid sausage and other processed meats since they are often high in fat.

Can I use ground meats on my low-fat diet?
Many ground meats are high in fat, but with a little care you can include them in your diet. When beef and pork are ground, fat often is included with the meat. And in the case of turkey, the skin sometimes is added. The trick is to always select the leanest ground beef, pork, or turkey, and drain well after cooking.

What kinds of poultry are best for my low-fat diet?
Choose chicken or turkey because they are low in fat. Avoid goose and duck, which are high in fat. Manufacturers of processed poultry products, such as bologna and frankfurters, often add fat. So, check the label before you buy these. They may contain as much fat as other processed meats.

What makes fish a good choice for a low-fat diet?
Fish has less saturated fat than either meat or poultry. For this reason, try to eat fish at least twice a week.

Is shellfish high in cholesterol?
Shrimp, crab, and oysters are relatively high in cholesterol, so choose these infrequently. Other shellfish, such as lobster, clams, and mussels, have lower cholesterol levels and can be eaten more freely.

How does cheese rate as a protein choice?
Cheese is an excellent source of protein, as well as calcium and other nutrients. But, it contains as much cholesterol as meat and more saturated fat than many meats. You can include some cheese in your diet, but try to select a type of cheese relatively low in fat.

Which cheeses are low in fat?
Choose a cheese that contains less than 6 grams of fat per ounce. Selecting a low-fat cheese can be quite confusing because there are so many kinds of cheese (part-skim, low-fat, imitation, process, natural, hard, and soft). Generally, natural and process cheeses are highest in saturated fat. Cheeses labeled 'low-fat' or 'imitation' often have less fat. But, even low-fat cheeses may have more saturated fat than many types of beef and pork.

How many eggs can I eat on a low-cholesterol diet?
Four per week is a good guideline. However, since all the cholesterol in eggs is found in the yolks, it's only the yolks you need to limit. Be sure to count egg yolks used in packaged and prepared foods. Read the labels on packaged foods so you can calculate these eggs into your daily tally. Since egg whites contain only a trace of fat and no cholesterol, you can eat all the egg whites you want.

What kind of milk should I buy?
Choose 1 percent or, even better, skim milk. Both contain the same nutrients as 2 percent and whole milk but much less fat, cholesterol, and calories.

If you don't like the taste of skim milk initially, try making a gradual change. Drink 2 percent milk for a few weeks, then move to 1 percent milk, and finally to skim milk.

What fruits and vegetables can I eat on a low-fat diet?
Most fresh or frozen fruits and vegetables contain no cholesterol, are low in fat and calories, and are rich in vitamins and minerals. As long as you don't

Numbers to Live By

Increase your odds for good health by sticking to these special numbers—30, 10, and 300. They apply to the following low-fat guidelines, recommended by several public health organizations for all adult Americans:

1) Consume no more than 30 percent of your total daily calories from fat.
2) Choose a daily diet with no more than 10 percent of your total calories (one-third of fat calories) from saturated fat. Also, consume no more than one-third of fat calories from polyunsaturated fat. Make up the remainder of your fat calories with monounsaturated fat.
3) Eat no more than 300 milligrams of cholesterol daily. Monitor the amount and forms of meat, dairy products, and other foods of animal origin in your diet.

combine them with high-fat foods, you can eat all the fruits and vegetables you want.

Avocados and olives are exceptions. Both are high in monounsaturated fat and should be eaten in moderation on a low-fat diet.

What kinds of bread should I buy?
White, whole wheat, pumpernickel, and rye breads are low in fat. For variety, pitas, bagels, English muffins, and rice cakes make good choices.

Pass up croissants, butter rolls, sweet rolls, Danish pastry, and doughnuts.

What should I look for in a breakfast cereal?
Your cereal should contain between 2 and 4 grams of fiber per serving. Fiber plays an important role in maintaining a healthy digestive tract and soluble fiber (such as that found in oat bran) may help lower blood cholesterol levels in some people. Less than 2 grams of fiber per serving will not have a

Computing Your Fat Calories

You'll need to do some calculations to determine the percentage of calories from fat in your food. But, once you know the equations, the rest is a piece of cake (angel cake, that is).

First, you need to know how many grams of fat are in the food and that 1 gram of fat contains 9 calories. You also need to know the number of calories in the food. Many package labels include this information. For nonpackaged foods, use a calorie handbook and the fat and cholesterol chart that begins on page 119. Then, simply plug the numbers into the equations below.

Step 1: Total fat in grams x 9 = total calories from fat
Step 2: (Total fat calories ÷ total calories) × 100 = % calories from fat

beneficial effect on the intestinal tract. More than 4 grams of fiber per serving can cause gastric distress.

How can pasta and rice fit into my low-fat diet?
Pasta and rice can round out a low-fat meal. Nutritionally they provide energy, and even some protein. Since some noodles and pasta are made with whole eggs, check the package label and avoid purchasing these products.

More and more food labels contain the words "no cholesterol." Can I eat these foods more freely?
Only if the food also is low in fat. "No cholesterol" labels can be deceiving. While these foods don't contain cholesterol, many of them are still high in fat. And, some of them may even contain saturated fats from plant sources (palm and coconut oils).

What should I choose for a low-fat dessert?
Fresh fruit can satisfy your sweet tooth, and at the same time provide vitamins and fiber. Angel cake is cholesterol-free and contains just a pinch of fat. In the frozen food case, look for frozen yogurt, sherbets, sorbets, and ice milk.

What about snack foods?
Low-fat crackers made without palm or coconut oil, matzo, breadsticks, saltines, zwieback, plain popcorn, and pretzels make great snacks. Crunchy raw vegetables or fresh fruits are other snack-time choices.

Fat-Slashing Cooking Tips

What is the best low-fat cooking method for meat, poultry, or fish?
To keep the fat low, broil, poach, bake, or roast these foods. Avoid frying them.

When you roast meat, place it on a rack so the fat drips away from it. Then, baste the meat with fat-free ingredients such as wine, tomato juice, or lemon juice instead of fatty drippings.

Can I use my microwave oven for low-fat cooking?
Microwave cooking works well on a low-fat diet. Since microwave cooking often keeps foods moister than conventional cooking, you'll need less fat.

How should I prepare my meat for cooking?
If you choose lean cuts, trim all the visible fat from the meat

before you cook it (see photo, above). If you are cooking ground meat, drain off the fat once you finish cooking.

If you're cooking poultry, remove the skin before you cook the meat.

What's the best type of fat to use for cooking?
To sauté foods, choose either a polyunsaturated or a mono-unsaturated cooking oil. Keep

in mind that a nonstick skillet and nonstick spray coating can help eliminate the need for any fat (see photo, above).

When selecting recipes for cookies, cakes, breads, and other baked foods, choose those that use either cooking oil or margarine. Avoid those that call for butter, hydrogentated shortening, or lard.

When a favorite casserole recipe calls for onion, green pepper, and celery cooked in butter, what can I do?
Cook the vegetables in a little water instead of the butter until tender. Then, drain the vegetables and continue as the recipe directs.

I always add fat to rice or pasta. Do I need to do this?
No. Our taste panels find rice acceptable without the added fat, especially when the rice is served with the meat course.

Also, skip adding oil to the water you cook your pasta in. After you drain the pasta, rinse it in hot water to prevent the pasta from sticking together.

If I shouldn't add butter to my vegetables, what can I use for seasoning?
Try sprinkling vegetables with lemon juice, flavored vinegars, or low-fat salad dressings. Garlic powder, herbs, and spices also perk up vegetable flavors.

Cutting Fat From Fried Chicken

Let's take a closer look at the fat-trimming techniques we used below. First, we chose oven-frying over deep-fat- or skillet-frying. This allowed us to cook the chicken with absolutely no additional fat. (As an added bonus, oven-frying is easier and less messy than conventional frying.) To further cut fat, we chose chicken breasts over legs or thighs because white meat contains less fat than dark meat. Then, we removed the skin before cooking. For the coating, we used cornflakes which contain neither fat nor cholesterol. Also, we found skim milk worked as well as an egg for making the crumbs stick. Our total fat savings: 7 grams.

Fried Chicken

4 g fat
72 mg cholesterol

We applied some fat-cutting tips to a traditional recipe for fried chicken, and reduced the fat per serving by 7 grams (from 11 to 4 grams).

2 whole large chicken breasts (about 2 pounds total), halved lengthwise

● Remove skin from the chicken breasts. Rinse chicken; pat dry with paper towels.

3 cups cornflakes
1 teaspoon dried sage, marjoram, *or* basil, crushed

● Finely crush the cornflakes. (You should have 1 cup.) Stir together cornflake crumbs and sage, marjoram, or basil; set aside.

2 tablespoons skim milk

● If desired, season chicken with salt and pepper. Brush chicken with milk. Roll chicken in crumb mixture, patting to coat each side evenly. Place chicken, meat side up, in a 13x9x2-inch baking dish.
  Bake in a 375° oven for 50 to 55 minutes or till tender. Makes 4 servings.

Nutrition information per serving: 216 calories, 1 g saturated fat, 1 g monounsaturated fat, 1 g polyunsaturated fat, 28 g protein, 15 g carbohydrate, 280 mg sodium, 238 mg potassium.

Cutting Fat From Pudding

A traditional chocolate pudding contains 9 grams of fat and 190 milligrams of cholesterol per serving. How did we lower fat to 1 gram and cholesterol to 3 milligrams?

First, we worked on reducing cholesterol by eliminating the eggs. Then, we developed an eggless pudding that tastes every bit as rich as the traditional recipe. To lower fat, we substituted skim milk for whole milk. Since cocoa powder is lower in fat than unsweetened chocolate squares, we opted for cocoa. Our total fat savings: 8 grams.

Chocolate Pudding

1 g fat
3 mg cholesterol

½ cup sugar
¼ cup unsweetened cocoa powder
3 tablespoons cornstarch
⅛ teaspoon salt

● In a heavy medium saucepan combine the sugar, unsweetened cocoa powder, cornstarch, and salt.

2½ cups skim milk
1½ teaspoons vanilla

● Stir in the milk. Cook and stir over medium heat till thickened and bubbly. Cook and stir for 2 minutes more. Remove from the heat. Stir in vanilla. Pour the pudding into a bowl. Cover the surface with clear plastic wrap. Chill thoroughly; do not stir. Makes 4 servings.

Nutrition information per serving: 186 calories, 1 g saturated fat, 0 g monounsaturated fat, 0 g polyunsaturated fat, 6 g protein, 40 g carbohydrate, 147 mg sodium, 317 mg potassium.

Menus

*T*o start you on the low-fat cooking track, we've combined some of our leanest and tastiest recipes into nutritious and delicious meals. The whole family will enjoy meals such as A Classic Menu built around Healthy Pot Roast, or Weekend Brunch featuring Corn-Oat Waffles and Turkey-Apple Sausage. Each menu includes two or more taste-tempting recipes and a countdown that guides you through each cooking step.

Planning Low-Fat Meals

On the next few pages, you'll find 11 flavorful, low-fat menus that we've planned for you. You also might want to do some of your own fat-shy meal planning. Here are some tips to help you in that healthy endeavor.

Budget Your Fat

Planning meals for your low-fat diet is like planning your household budget. Within your budget, you have a limited amount of money to spend on luxury items. On your diet, you have a limited number of calories to spend on fat.

Remember your goal—keep daily fat calories to 30 percent or less of daily total calories.

Examine the foods you eat during the entire day. If you go overboard on fat at one meal, take extra care to keep your next meal lean.

Planning Menus

Once you start creating menus, get out a pencil and paper and write them down. As you list the different foods, calculate the percentage of fat calories for each item (see tip, page 5).

After-Work Menu

Sweet and Sour Turkey

Millet Pilaf

Tossed salad

Dinner rolls

Ice milk and strawberries

Eliminate those foods that take you over your fat or cholesterol limit.

Meal-Planning Steps

The following steps will help you plan balanced, nutritious meals for you and your family.
● Start by selecting the main dish. You'll spend most of your fat calories on the meat, poultry, or fish that you choose.

● Add a bread or cereal. Remember that any margarine or fat you serve with your bread will count as fat calories.
● Choose a hot or cold vegetable. Go easy on sauces, margarine, and toppings. They all can add fat calories.
● Add a salad, but watch the dressing! Even calorie-reduced dressings can take you over the brink quickly.

● Select a beverage. Skim milk adds calcium and lots of other nutrients, but little fat.
● Look over your meal. Can you afford a dessert? If you can, make a low-fat selection such as angel cake, frozen yogurt, or ice milk. If you have used up your fat calories, skip dessert or opt for fresh fruit.

After-Work Dinner

Does low-fat eating seem out of the question when you're short on time? The trick to having a wonderful low-fat dinner on the table quickly is to choose a fast-cooking meat and to dovetail your cooking steps. To see how this works, follow the cooking steps given here to make every minute count.

Menu

Sweet and Sour Turkey
Millet Pilaf
Tossed salad
Dinner rolls
Ice milk and strawberries

Menu Countdown

30 Minutes Ahead: Prepare *Millet Pilaf;* let simmer. Brown turkey steaks for *Sweet and Sour Turkey.*
20 Minutes Ahead: Add sauce to turkey in the skillet. Wash and slice strawberries for dessert; place in the refrigerator.
15 Minutes Ahead: Set the table. Prepare the tossed salad. Arrange rolls in a basket.
5 Minutes Ahead: Thicken sauce for turkey, then stir in pea pods and oranges.
To serve: Pour sauce over turkey steaks.

Millet Pilaf

1 g fat
0 mg cholesterol

Simmer a mix of rice and millet in chicken broth for rich flavor. (Pictured on pages 10–11.)

1½ **cups chicken broth**
1 **cup water**
½ **cup millet**
½ **cup long grain rice**

● In a 2-quart saucepan combine chicken broth and water. Bring to boiling. Stir in millet and rice. Return to boiling; reduce heat. Simmer, covered, for 15 to 20 minutes or till rice is tender. Remove from the heat.

¼ **cup sliced green onion**
 Green onion fan (optional)

● Stir green onion into the millet mixture. Let stand, covered, for 5 minutes. Fluff with a fork before serving. If desired, garnish with green onion fan. Makes 4 servings.

Nutrition information per serving: 147 calories, 0 g saturated fat, 0 g polyunsaturated fat, 0 g monounsaturated fat, 5 g protein, 29 g carbohydrate, 292 mg sodium, 172 mg potassium.

Sweet and Sour Turkey

1 g fat
0 mg cholesterol

Pineapple lends the sweet and red wine vinegar gives the sour to the subtly flavored sauce. (Pictured on pages 10–11.)

Nonstick spray coating
4 turkey breast tenderloin steaks, cut ½ inch thick (about 1 pound)

● Spray a *cold* large skillet with nonstick coating. Preheat skillet over medium heat, then add turkey steaks. Cook over medium heat for 5 to 7 minutes or till turkey is light brown, turning steaks once.

½ of a 6-ounce can (⅓ cup) frozen pineapple juice concentrate, thawed
¼ cup water
¼ cup red wine vinegar
1 tablespoon soy sauce
¼ teaspoon garlic powder
¼ teaspoon ground ginger

● Meanwhile, for sauce, in a small bowl stir together pineapple juice concentrate, water, vinegar, soy sauce, garlic powder, and ginger.

● Add sauce to skillet. Bring to boiling; reduce heat. Simmer, covered, for 12 to 15 minutes or till turkey is no longer pink. Transfer turkey steaks to a serving platter. Cover to keep warm.

2 tablespoons cold water
1 tablespoon cornstarch

● In a custard cup stir together water and cornstarch. Stir mixture into sauce in the skillet. Cook and stir over medium heat till the mixture is thickened and bubbly.

1 11-ounce can mandarin orange sections, drained
1 6-ounce package frozen pea pods
Tomato wedges (optional)

● Stir orange sections and frozen pea pods into mixture in the skillet. Cook and stir about 2 minutes or till heated through. Spoon oranges, pea pods, and sauce over turkey steaks. Garnish with tomato wedges, if desired. Makes 4 servings.

Nutrition information per serving: 226 calories, 0 g saturated fat, 0 g polyunsaturated fat, 0 g monounsaturated fat, 28 g protein, 27 g carbohydrate, 308 mg sodium, 512 mg potassium.

Speedy Lunch for Two

For a lunch in short order, try this soup and sandwich menu. You can keep most of the ingredients for both *Easy Vegetable Soup* and *Dilled Tuna Sandwiches* on the shelf. The zesty soup combines stewed tomatoes, pasta, frozen vegetables, and oregano. For the tuna salad filling reduced-calorie cucumber salad dressing takes the place of high-fat, high-cholesterol mayonnnaise. Follow our countdown and you can have lunch on the table in 15 minutes.

Menu

Easy Vegetable Soup
Dilled Tuna Sandwiches
Fresh Fruit

Menu Countdown

1 Day Ahead: Put the salad dressing and tuna in the refrigerator to chill.
15 Minutes Ahead: Combine the tomato mixture for the soup. Place on the stove and bring to boiling. Drain the tuna for the sandwiches in a colander. Rinse and drain lettuce leaves. Cut up the fresh fruit, if necessary; chill.
10 Minutes Ahead: Add the vegetables and pasta to the soup. Cut up the cucumber and radishes for the tuna filling.
5 Minutes Ahead: Prepare the *Dilled Tuna Sandwiches.*
To Serve: Cut the sandwiches in half and place on plates. Ladle soup into bowls. Sprinkle with the Parmesan cheese.

Dilled Tuna Sandwiches

**9 g fat
48 mg cholesterol**

Crisp cucumber and radishes add crunch to the tuna salad filling.

3 **tablespoons reduced-calorie creamy cucumber salad dressing**
¼ **teaspoon dried dillweed**
⅛ **teaspoon pepper**
½ **cup chopped seeded cucumber**
2 **tablespoons chopped radishes**
1 **6½-ounce can tuna (water pack), drained and broken into chunks**

● In a medium mixing bowl combine salad dressing, dillweed, and pepper. Stir in chopped cucumber and radishes. Add drained tuna. Toss gently to mix.

2 **lettuce leaves**
4 **slices pumpernickel, rye, *or* whole wheat bread**

● For each sandwich, place one lettuce leaf on a slice of bread. Top with half of the tuna mixture and another slice of bread. Serves 2.

Nutrition information per serving: 340 calories, 1 g saturated fat, 1 g monounsaturated fat, 1 g polyunsaturated fat, 32 g protein, 34 g carbohydrate, 909 mg sodium, 653 mg potassium.

Easy Vegetable Soup

1 g fat
2 mg cholesterol

Orzo, also called rosamarina, is a tiny rice-shaped pasta. Look for it on the pasta shelf.

1 8-ounce can stewed tomatoes
½ cup tomato juice
¼ cup water
½ teaspoon sugar
½ teaspoon dried basil, crushed
¼ teaspoon dried oregano, crushed
Dash garlic powder

● In a medium saucepan combine stewed tomatoes, tomato juice, water, sugar, basil, oregano, and garlic powder. Cook over medium-high heat till boiling.

½ cup loose-pack frozen broccoli, cauliflower, and carrots *or* other frozen mixed vegetables
2 tablespoons orzo
1 tablespoon grated Parmesan cheese

● Stir frozen vegetables and orzo into the tomato mixture. Return to boiling. Reduce heat. Simmer, covered, about 10 minutes or till vegetables and pasta are tender.
    To serve, ladle into 2 bowls. Sprinkle with Parmesan cheese. Makes 2 servings.

Nutrition information per serving: 97 calories, 1 g saturated fat, 0 g monounsaturated fat, 0 g polyunsaturated fat, 4 g protein, 20 g carbohydrate, 589 mg sodium, 235 mg potassium.

For Sodium Watchers

As Americans have become more sodium conscious, many food processors have responded by producing sodium-reduced canned tomatoes, tomato juice, canned tuna, soy sauce, cheese, and other products. If you're concerned about sodium in your diet, you may want to use these products.
    Whatever the product, any food bearing a nutrition label will list sodium.

In addition, foods that make a sodium claim must fall within these guidelines:
Sodium free: The product contains no more than 5 milligrams of sodium in each serving.
Very low sodium: The product contains no more than 35 milligrams per serving.
Low sodium: The product contains no more than 140 milligrams per serving.
Reduced sodium: Sodium levels have been reduced by at least 75 percent from the original product.
No salt added: The food processor has not added any salt. However, such a product may be naturally high in sodium.

A Classic Menu

This stick-to-the-ribs meal celebrates homestyle cooking. *Healthy Pot Roast* features tender beef, potatoes, leeks, and carrots in a tomato sauce. A basket of *Molasses-Oat Rolls* and our fresh-tasting *Green Goddess Salad* complete the meal. For dessert, delight in cool and creamy *Apricot Sherbet.*

Menu

Healthy Pot Roast

Molasses-Oat Rolls

Green Goddess Salad

Apricot Sherbet

A Classic Menu

Menu

Healthy Pot Roast
Molasses-Oat Rolls *(see recipe, page 20)*
Green Goddess Salad
Apricot Sherbet *(see recipe, page 21)*

Menu Countdown

24 to 9 hours Ahead: Mix the ingre–dients for the *Apricot Sherbet* and freeze about 3 hours. Then, beat the sherbet and freeze till serving time.
3 Hours Ahead: Mix the dough for *Molasses-Oat Rolls.* Set aside to rise. Make the dressing for *Green Goddess Salad;* chill till serving time.
2 Hours Ahead: Brown the meat for *Healthy Pot Roast.* Add the tomato mixture and let simmer.
1½ Hours Ahead: Prepare the salad ingredients. Shape rolls.
40 Minutes Ahead: Add vegetables to pot roast. Set the table.
15 Minutes Ahead: Bake the rolls.
5 Minutes Ahead: Transfer meat and vegetables for pot roast to platter. Cover with foil to keep warm. Make the gravy.
To Serve: Add dressing to salad. Transfer rolls to a basket. Spoon gravy over meat and vegetables.

Green Goddess Salad

1 g fat
4 mg cholesterol

We slimmed down a classic Green Goddess salad dressing with low-fat yogurt and cottage cheese. (Pictured on pages 16–17.)

½ **cup plain low-fat yogurt**
½ **cup low-fat cottage cheese**
⅓ **cup parsley sprigs**
1 **green onion, sliced**
1 **clove garlic, minced**
2 **teaspoons anchovy paste**
½ **teaspoon Worcestershire sauce**
¼ **teaspoon dried basil, crushed**
⅛ **teaspoon dry mustard**

● For dressing, in a blender container or food processor bowl combine yogurt, cottage cheese, parsley, green onion, garlic, anchovy paste, Worcestershire sauce, basil, and mustard. Cover; blend or process till smooth. Chill in a tightly covered jar at least 2 hours.

6 **cups torn mixed greens**
1 **large tomato, cut into wedges**
½ **medium cucumber, sliced**

● For salad, in a salad bowl combine greens, tomato, and cucumber. Drizzle dressing over salad. Makes 6 servings.

Nutrition information per serving: 50 calories, 1 g saturated fat, 0 g monounsaturated fat, 0 g polyunsaturated fat, 5 g protein, 5 g carbohydrate, 115 mg sodium, 301 mg potassium.

Healthy Pot Roast

8 g fat
72 mg cholesterol

Our fat-cutting tricks—start with a lean eye of round or rump roast and replace the traditional gravy with a robust tomato sauce. (Pictured on pages 16–17.)

| 1 | 1½-pound boneless beef eye of round roast *or* round rump roast |
| | Nonstick spray coating |

● Trim fat from meat. Spray a *cold* Dutch oven with nonstick coating, and preheat it over medium-high heat. Brown beef on all sides in the Dutch oven.

1	14½-ounce can stewed tomatoes
1	medium onion, chopped (½ cup)
½	cup tomato juice
2	bay leaves
1	clove garlic, minced
1	teaspoon instant beef bouillon granules
1	teaspoon dried basil, crushed
⅛	teaspoon pepper

● Add stewed tomatoes, onion, tomato juice, bay leaves, garlic, beef bouillon granules, basil, and pepper. Bring to boiling; reduce heat. Simmer, covered, for 1 hour.

12	whole tiny new potatoes *or* 3 medium potatoes
3	medium carrots, cut into 1-inch pieces
2	leeks, sliced, *or* 1 large onion, sliced

● Meanwhile, for the tiny potatoes, remove a narrow strip of peel from the center of each. For the medium potatoes, peel and cut each potato into quarters.

Add potatoes, carrots, and leeks or onion to the Dutch oven. Simmer, covered, for 30 to 40 minutes more or till meat and vegetables are tender. Discard bay leaves. Transfer meat and vegetables to a serving platter; keep warm.

| 2 | tablespoons cold water |
| 4 | teaspoons cornstarch |

● For gravy, measure the pan juices. If necessary, add enough water to make 1¼ cups. Return pan juices to the Dutch oven. In a small bowl stir together water and cornstarch. Add cornstarch mixture to juices. Cook and stir till mixture is thickened and bubbly. Cook and stir for 2 minutes more. Spoon some of the gravy over meat and vegetables. Pass remaining gravy. Makes 6 servings.

Nutrition information per serving: 284 calories, 3 g saturated fat, 3 g monounsaturated fat, 0 g polyunsaturated fat, 27 g protein, 27 g carbohydrate, 470 mg sodium, 663 mg potassium.

Molasses-Oat Rolls

3 g fat
0 mg cholesterol

These fiber-rich rolls contain both oat bran and whole wheat flour. (Pictured on pages 16–17.)

1 cup all-purpose flour
1 package active dry yeast

● In a small mixing bowl combine all-purpose flour and yeast. Set aside.

¾ cup skim milk
¼ cup molasses
2 tablespoons cooking oil
1 teaspoon salt

● In a small saucepan combine skim milk, molasses, cooking oil, and salt. Heat just till warm (120° to 130°), stirring constantly. Add the milk mixture to the flour mixture. Beat with an electric mixer on low to medium speed for 30 seconds, scraping bowl constantly. Beat on high speed for 3 minutes.

½ cup oat bran
1¼ to 1¾ cups whole wheat flour

● Using a spoon, stir in oat bran. Then, stir in as much whole wheat flour as you can. Turn dough out onto lightly floured surface. Knead in enough remaining whole wheat flour to make a moderately stiff dough that is smooth and elastic (6 to 8 minutes total). Shape into a ball. Place in a lightly greased bowl; turn once to grease surface. Cover; let rise in a warm place till double (about 1½ hours).

Nonstick spray coating

● Punch dough down. Turn out onto a lightly floured surface. Divide dough in half. Cover; let rest for 10 minutes.
  Meanwhile, spray a large baking sheet with nonstick coating. Divide each half of the dough into 6 pieces. Shape each piece into a ball, pulling the edges under to make a smooth top. Place about 2 inches apart on the baking sheet. Cover; let rise in a warm place till nearly double (40 to 45 minutes).
  Bake in a 375° oven for 10 to 12 minutes or till light brown. Makes 12 rolls.

Nutrition information per roll: 130 calories, 0 g saturated fat, 1 g monounsaturated fat, 2 g polyunsaturated fat, 4 g protein, 24 g carbohydrate, 188 mg sodium, 175 mg potassium.

Apricot Sherbet

1 g fat
3 mg cholesterol

Cool on your tongue; tangy on your taste buds. (Pictured on pages 16–17.)

2 cups low-fat buttermilk
1 12-ounce can apricot cake and
**   pastry filling**

● In a medium mixing bowl stir together buttermilk and cake and pastry filling. Pour the mixture into an 8x4x2-inch loaf pan. Freeze about 3 hours or till firm.

● Break frozen buttermilk mixture into chunks. Transfer to a chilled large mixing bowl. Beat with an electric mixer on medium to high speed till smooth but not melted. Return to cold pan. Cover and freeze 6 hours or till firm. To serve, scoop into dessert dishes. Serves 6.

Nutrition information per serving: 129 calories, 0 g saturated fat, 0 g monounsaturated fat, 0 g polyunsaturated fat, 3 g protein, 28 g carbohydrate, 99 mg sodium, 124 mg potassium.

Buying Margarine

Perplexed about which margarine to buy? Once you know what to look for, the decision becomes easy.

Generally, the softer the margarine, the less saturated fat it contains. But this is not a clear guideline, so be sure to check the ingredient list on the label. The first ingredient listed should be *liquid* vegetable oil, such as corn, safflower, or soybean oil.

Then, look at the "nutrition information per serving" to determine the P/S ratio—the ratio of polyunsaturated to saturated fat. You want a margarine that has a P/S ratio of at least 2 to 1, or at least twice as much polyunsaturated fat as saturated fat. For example, a margarine that contains 4 grams of polyunsaturated fat and 2 grams of saturated fat would be a good choice.

In addition, consider how you will use the margarine. For baked foods, choose a stick margarine. For table use, a tub or liquid squeeze margarine may be your better choice.

A Special-Occasion Dinner

For entertaining, surprise your friends with this menu that's low in fat and can be ready in less than an hour. The main course, *Pork with Mushrooms,* features tender pork medaillons and mushrooms in a tangy yogurt sauce. And, this rich-tasting entrée contains only 4 grams of fat per serving. *Vegetable Medley* features herbed brussels sprouts and carrots. For dessert, serve our *Maple Apples* stuffed with dried fruit bits or raisins.

Menu

Pork with Mushrooms
Fettuccine
Vegetable Medley
Maple Apples

Menu Countdown

55 Minutes Ahead: Preheat the oven.
50 Minutes Ahead: Prepare and bake the *Maple Apples.*
40 Minutes Ahead: Set the table.
30 Minutes Ahead: Cut and pound the pork. Cut up the mushrooms and green onions for the pork recipe. Assemble the remaining ingredients for *Pork with Mushrooms* and *Vegetable Medley.*
20 Minutes Ahead: Fill the pasta pan with water. Bring to boiling.
15 Minutes Ahead: Prepare the *Vegetable Medley.* Let simmer while you cook the *Pork with Mushrooms.* Add the fettuccine to the boiling water.
Just Before Serving: Remove apples from the oven, and let them cool slightly while you eat.

Vegetable Medley

1 g fat
1 mg cholesterol

Brussels sprouts and carrots contrast in color and shape, making a pretty, as well as a tasty, vegetable dish.

1 **10-ounce package frozen brussels sprouts**
1 **10-ounce package frozen tiny whole carrots**
3 **tablespoons reduced-calorie Italian salad dressing**

● In a large saucepan combine brussels sprouts, carrots, and ½ cup *water.* Bring to boiling; reduce heat. Simmer, covered, for 8 to 10 minutes or till vegetables are crisp-tender. Drain vegetables. Return to saucepan. Add salad dressing. Toss to coat. Cook 1 minute more or till heated through. Makes 4 servings.

Nutrition information per serving: 61 calories, 0 g saturated fat, 0 g monounsaturated fat, 0 g polyunsaturated fat, 3 g protein, 12 g carbohydrate, 147 mg sodium, 344 mg potassium.

 Microwave Directions: Run cold water over frozen vegetables to separate. Cut any large brussels sprouts in half. In a microwave-safe 1½-quart casserole micro-cook brussels sprouts, carrots, and 1 tablespoon water, covered on 100% power (high) for 9 to 11 minutes or till crisp-tender, stirring twice. Drain; return to casserole. Add salad dressing; toss to coat. Cook, covered, for ½ to 1 minute more or till heated through.

Pork with Mushrooms

4 g fat
61 mg cholesterol

The fat-busters in this recipe are skim milk and yogurt. They add creaminess to the mushroom sauce, but keep the fat and cholesterol levels low.

¾ **pound whole pork tenderloin**
Nonstick spray coating

● Trim fat from pork. Cut pork crosswise into 8 slices. For each slice, place between two sheets of clear plastic wrap. Using the flat side of a meat mallet, pound to ¼-inch thickness.

Spray a *cold* large skillet with nonstick coating. Preheat skillet. Add pork and cook over medium-high heat about 3 minutes or till browned. Turn and cook for 2 to 4 minutes more or till no pink remains. Remove from skillet; keep warm.

1 **cup sliced fresh mushrooms**
¼ **cup sliced green onion**
1 **clove garlic, minced**

● Add mushrooms, green onion, and garlic to skillet. Cook and stir over medium heat till vegetables are tender.

½ **cup plain low-fat yogurt**
⅓ **cup skim milk**
1 **tablespoon all-purpose flour**
1 **teaspoon instant chicken bouillon granules**
⅛ **teaspoon ground nutmeg**
⅛ **teaspoon pepper**

● Stir together yogurt, milk, flour, bouillon granules, nutmeg, and pepper. (Mixture may look curdled.) Add to mushroom mixture. Cook and stir till thickened and bubbly. Return meat to skillet and cook for 2 minutes more or till heated through. Makes 4 servings.

Nutrition information per serving: 149 calories, 1 g saturated fat, 2 g monounsaturated fat, 0 g polyunsaturated fat, 21 g protein, 6 g carbohydrate, 299 mg sodium, 530 mg potassium.

Maple Apples

0 g fat
0 mg cholesterol

Besides being a naturally low-fat dessert, apples contain soluble fiber, which may help lower blood cholesterol levels.

4 **medium baking apples**

● Core apples and peel off a strip around top of each. Place in an 8x8x2-inch baking dish.

4 **tablespoons mixed dried fruit bits**
or **raisins**
⅓ **cup maple-flavored syrup**

● Spoon *1 tablespoon* dried fruit bits or raisins into center of *each* apple. Spoon syrup over apples, letting syrup run to bottom of dish. Cover with foil.

Bake in a 350° oven for 40 to 45 minutes or till apples are tender. Cool slightly and serve warm or chill and serve cold. To serve, spoon liquid in dish over apples. Makes 4 servings.

Nutrition information per serving: 186 calories, 0 g saturated fat, 0 g monounsaturated fat, 0 g polyunsaturated fat, 1 g protein, 49 g carbohydrate, 20 mg sodium, 233 mg potassium.

Holiday Dinner

Celebrate the holidays with traditional fare designed for today's lifestyles. *Holiday Turkey Bundles* taste like turkey, dressing, and gravy without the time and trouble involved in cooking a whole bird. Round out the menu with all the trimmings.

Menu

Holiday Turkey Bundles
with Chicken Gravy

Candied Sweet Potatoes

Cranberry Sauce

Whole wheat rolls

Pumpkin Pie

Whipped Topping
(optional)

Holiday Dinner

Menu

Holiday Turkey Bundles with
  Chicken Gravy
Candied Sweet Potatoes
  (see recipe, page 28)
Cranberry Sauce *(see recipe, page 28)*
Whole wheat rolls
Pumpkin Pie *(see recipe, page 29)*
Whipped Topping (optional)
  (see recipe, page 39)

Menu Countdown

1 Day Ahead: Make *Pumpkin Pie;* chill.
Make *Cranberry Sauce;* chill.
2 Hours Ahead: Boil the fresh sweet
potatoes for *Candied Sweet Potatoes.*
Set table.
1 Hour Ahead: Prepare dressing for
Holiday Turkey Bundles.
45 Minutes Ahead: Peel potatoes and
assemble *Candied Sweet Potatoes.*
40 Minutes Ahead: Place potatoes in
oven to bake. Assemble *Holiday Turkey
Bundles,* then bake.
15 Minutes Ahead: Prepare *Chicken
Gravy.*
At dessert time: Prepare *Whipped
Topping,* if desired.

Chicken Gravy

0 g fat
2 mg cholesterol

You can indulge in gravy often with this no-fat version.

1 12-ounce can evaporated skim milk
**2 teaspoons instant chicken bouillon
   granules**
⅛ teaspoon pepper

● In a small saucepan stir together *1⅓ cups*
of the evaporated milk, the chicken bouillon
granules, and pepper.

2 tablespoons all-purpose flour

● Stir the remaining milk and flour together till
well blended. Stir flour mixture into mixture in
the saucepan. Cook and stir over medium heat
till thickened and bubbly. Cook and stir for 1
minute more. Makes 6 (¼-cup) servings.

Nutrition information per serving: 57 calories, 0 g saturated fat,
0 g polyunsaturated fat, 0 g monounsaturated fat, 5 g protein,
9 g carbohydrate, 365 mg sodium, 191 mg potassium.

Holiday Turkey Bundles

2 g fat
2 mg cholesterol

Accent the moist dressing with either poultry seasoning or sage. (Pictured on pages 24–25.)

½ cup water
½ cup chopped celery
¼ cup chopped onion
½ teaspoon poultry seasoning
   or dried sage, crushed
¼ teaspoon instant chicken
   bouillon granules

● In a small saucepan combine water, celery, onion, poultry seasoning or sage, and bouillon granules. Bring to boiling; reduce heat. Simmer, covered, about 5 minutes or till celery is tender. Remove from the heat.

4 cups dry bread cubes (6 to 8 slices)
   Nonstick spray coating

● For dressing, place bread cubes in a large mixing bowl. Pour vegetable mixture over bread cubes. Toss gently to mix. Spray a 12x7½x2-inch baking dish with nonstick coating. Transfer dressing to the baking dish.

1 10-ounce package frozen asparagus
   spears
6 turkey breast slices (about ¾ pound)
1 tablespoon white wine
   Worcestershire sauce

● Cook asparagus in a small amount of boiling water for 5 to 7 minutes or till crisp-tender. Drain well.
   Place *one-sixth* of the asparagus spears crosswise onto *each* turkey slice. Roll up turkey slices. Place turkey rolls, seam side down, on top of dressing. Brush turkey with white wine Worcestershire sauce. Bake, covered, in a 350° oven for 30 to 35 minutes or till turkey is tender and no longer pink.

Chicken Gravy (see recipe, opposite)
Paprika

● Meanwhile, prepare Chicken Gravy; spoon over turkey bundles. Sprinkle with paprika. Makes 6 servings.

Nutrition information per serving: 224 calories, 1 g saturated fat, 1 g polyunsaturated fat, 1 g monounsaturated fat, 22 g protein, 28 g carbohydrate, 633 mg sodium, 494 mg potassium.

Turkey Talk

Selecting the turkey cut called for in a recipe may be confusing because there are so many new products on the market. Use these brief descriptions to identify the different cuts.
   Turkey breast tenderloin is the whole muscle on the inside of the breast. *Turkey breast tenderloin steaks* are cut lengthwise from the tenderloin. They are usually ½ inch thick and resemble a fish fillet.
   Turkey breast steaks are cut crosswise from the breast. They are usually ½ to 1 inch thick. The ½-inch-thick steaks are interchangeable with boned skinless chicken breast halves of the same weight.
   Turkey breast slices or cutlets are also cut crosswise from the breast but are thinner than the steaks (usually ¼ to ⅜ inch thick). They can be used in recipes that call for pounded skinless, boneless, chicken breast halves.

Candied Sweet Potatoes

1 g fat
0 mg cholesterol

Glazed with apple juice, brown sugar, and cinnamon. (Pictured on pages 24–25.)

2 pounds sweet potatoes (4 *or* 5 medium) *or* two 18-ounce cans sweet potatoes, drained

● In a large saucepan cook fresh sweet potatoes, covered, in boiling water for 30 to 40 minutes or till tender. Drain. When cool enough to handle, peel and cut into ½-inch-thick slices. (*Or,* drain canned sweet potatoes and cut into ½-inch-thick slices.)

1 medium apple, cored and sliced
½ cup packed brown sugar
⅛ teaspoon ground cinnamon
Dash salt
2 tablespoons apple juice
Crab apple leaves (optional)

● In an 8x8x2-inch baking dish combine the sweet potato slices and apple slices. Sprinkle with brown sugar, cinnamon, and salt. Drizzle with apple juice. Bake, covered, in a 350° oven for 35 to 40 minutes or till heated through, occasionally stirring gently to distribute glaze. Garnish with a sprig of crab apple leaves, if desired. Makes 6 servings.

Nutrition information per serving: 244 calories, 0 g saturated fat, 0 g polyunsaturated fat, 0 g monounsaturated fat, 2 g protein, 59 g carbohydrate, 50 mg sodium, 374 mg potassium.

 Microwave Directions: Scrub fresh sweet potatoes thoroughly. Pat dry. Prick skin in several places. *Do not rub with shortening, margarine, or butter.* On a microwave-safe plate arrange potatoes in spoke fashion. Micro-cook, uncovered, on 100% power (high) for 10 to 14 minutes or till tender, rearranging once. Let stand 5 minutes. Peel and cut into ½-inch-thick slices. (*Or,* drain canned sweet potatoes and cut into ½-inch-thick slices.)

In a microwave-safe 8x8x2-inch baking dish combine sweet potato slices and apple slices. Sprinkle with brown sugar, cinnamon, and salt. Drizzle with apple juice. Cover with vented microwave-safe plastic wrap. Cook on high for 6 to 9 minutes or till heated through, stirring once. Garnish with crab apple leaves, if desired.

Cranberry Sauce

0 g fat
0 mg cholesterol

1 cup sugar
1 cup water

● In a medium saucepan combine sugar and water. Bring to boiling, stirring to dissolve sugar. Boil rapidly for 5 minutes.

2 cups cranberries (8 ounces)

● Add cranberries to sugar mixture. Return to boiling; reduce heat. Boil gently over medium-high heat for 3 to 4 minutes or till cranberry skins pop, stirring occasionally. Remove from the heat. Serve warm or chilled. Makes eight (¼-cup) servings.

Nutrition information per serving: 110 calories, 0 g saturated fat, 0 g polyunsaturated fat, 0 g monounsaturated fat, 0 g protein, 29 g carbohydrate, 1 mg sodium, 21 mg potassium.

Pumpkin Pie

6 g fat
1 mg cholesterol

Switching to all egg whites in the filling reduces the cholesterol without sacrificing the flavor. (Pictured on pages 24–25.)

1¼ **cups all-purpose flour**
⅛ **teaspoon salt**
¼ **cup cooking oil**
3 **tablespoons cold skim milk**
1 **to 2 teaspoons cold skim milk**

● In a medium mixing bowl stir together flour and salt. Combine oil and the 3 tablespoons milk; *do not stir.* Add all at once to flour mixture. Stir lightly with a fork to moisten. If necessary, stir in additional milk, *½ teaspoon* at a time, till moistened. Form into a ball. Flatten slightly with hands.

Cut two 12-inch squares of waxed paper. Place ball of dough between squares of waxed paper. Roll dough from center to the edges into a circle to edges of paper. Peel off top paper. Fit pastry, paper-side up, into a 9-inch pie plate. Remove waxed paper. Trim and flute edge. Set aside.

1 **16-ounce can pumpkin**
⅔ **cup packed brown sugar *or* sugar**
1½ **teaspoons ground cinnamon**
¼ **teaspoon ground ginger**
¼ **teaspoon ground nutmeg**
4 **egg whites**
1¼ **cups skim milk**

● In a large mixing bowl combine pumpkin, sugar, cinnamon, ginger, and nutmeg. Add egg whites. With a fork, beat mixture till combined. Stir in milk.

Place the pastry-lined pie plate on an oven rack. Pour in pumpkin mixture. Cover edge of pie with foil. Bake in a 375° oven for 25 minutes. Remove foil. Bake for 25 to 30 minutes more or till a knife inserted off-center comes out clean. Cool on a wire rack.

**Whipped Topping
(see recipe, page 39)
(optional)**

● Cover and chill pie to store. Serve topped with Whipped Topping, if desired. Makes 10 servings.

Nutrition information per serving: 192 calories, 1 g saturated fat, 3 g polyunsaturated fat, 1 g monounsaturated fat, 5 g protein, 31 g carbohydrate, 68 mg sodium, 187 mg potassium.

To keep the waxed paper from slipping while rolling out the pastry, sprinkle a little water on the work surface.

A Fresh Fish Supper

When you're watching fat and cholesterol, fish makes an excellent choice. And, that's especially true of flounder and sole, two of the leanest fish. To simplify meal preparation, the fish and vegetable cook together in *Broccoli-Flounder Rolls*. Just add *Herbed Brown Rice* and a tossed salad and you have a deliciously satisfying supper.

Menu

Broccoli-Flounder Rolls
Herbed Brown Rice
Tossed salad with reduced-calorie dressing

Menu Countdown

1 Day Ahead: If using frozen fish, put the fish in the refrigerator to thaw.
45 Minutes Ahead: Start cooking the *Herbed Brown Rice.*
35 Minutes Ahead: Prepare the stuffing for the fish rolls.
30 Minutes Ahead: Preheat the oven.
25 Minutes Ahead: Assemble fish rolls. (If you choose the microwave method, you can wait till 10 minutes before you want to eat to do this.)
20 Minutes Ahead: Put the fish rolls in the oven. Prepare the tossed salad while the fish bakes.

Herbed Brown Rice

1 g fat
0 mg cholesterol

Long grain rice works well in this recipe, too. Just cut the cooking time to 15 minutes.

1⅓ **cups water**
⅔ **cup regular brown rice**
¼ **cup chopped green pepper**
1 **teaspoon instant chicken bouillon granules**
½ **teaspoon dried basil, crushed**

● In a medium saucepan combine water, rice, green pepper, bouillon granules, and basil. Bring to boiling; reduce heat. Simmer, covered, for 30 to 40 minutes or till rice is tender.

1 **medium tomato, chopped**

● Stir in the chopped tomato. Heat through. Makes 4 servings.

Nutrition information per serving: 122 calories, 0 g saturated fat, 0 g monounsaturated fat, 0 g polyunsaturated fat, 3 g protein, 26 g carbohydrate, 231 mg sodium, 149 mg potassium.

Broccoli-Flounder Rolls

2 g fat
60 mg cholesterol

Lemon peel, lemon pepper, and Parmesan cheese perk up the flavor of the broccoli and mushroom stuffing.

4 fresh *or* frozen flounder, pike, *or* sole skinless fillets (about 1 pound)

● Thaw fish, if frozen. Rinse and pat dry with paper towels.

1½ cups loose-pack frozen cut broccoli
½ cup sliced fresh mushrooms
2 tablespoons grated Parmesan cheese
1 tablespoon diced pimiento
½ teaspoon finely shredded lemon peel
¼ teaspoon onion powder
¼ teaspoon lemon pepper

● For stuffing, place broccoli in a colander. Run cold water over broccoli till just thawed. Drain well. Chop the broccoli into small pieces.
  In a medium mixing bowl combine broccoli, mushrooms, Parmesan cheese, pimiento, lemon peel, onion powder, and lemon pepper.

Paprika

● Place about ½ *cup* of the stuffing on one end of *each* fillet. Roll fish around stuffing. Fasten securely with wooden toothpicks. Place the fish rolls, seam side down, in an 8x8x2-inch baking dish. Cover with foil.
  Bake in a 375° oven about 20 minutes or till fish just flakes with a fork. Transfer rolls to a serving platter. Sprinkle with paprika. Serves 4.

Nutrition information per serving: 134 calories, 1 g saturated fat, 0 g monounsaturated fat, 0 g polyunsaturated fat, 24 g protein, 5 g carbohydrate, 153 mg sodium, 455 mg potassium.

 Microwave directions: Assemble the fish rolls as directed above. Arrange fish rolls, seam side down, in a microwave-safe 8x8x2-inch baking dish. Cover with vented microwave-safe clear plastic wrap.

Micro-cook on 100% power (high) for 5 to 7 minutes or till fish just flakes with a fork, giving the dish a half-turn once. Transfer fish rolls to a serving platter. Sprinkle with paprika.

When the Fat Doesn't Add Up

You've probably noticed that the grams of saturated, monounsaturated, and polyunsaturated fat listed in our recipes often fail to equal the grams of total fat.

This occurs because we've rounded the numbers to the nearest whole gram. For example, a serving of *Broccoli-Flounder Rolls* contains 0.814 gram saturated fat, 0.495 gram monounsaturated fat, and 0.436 gram polyunsaturated fat. We rounded the saturated fat up to 1 gram and the monounsaturated and polyunsaturated fat down to 0 grams.

31

Weekend Brunch

The weekend's here! So, celebrate with this spectacular brunch. Start with a sip of *Mulled Citrus Cider*. Then, dig into a crispy *Corn-Oat Waffle*. Round out your meal with lean *Turkey-Apple Sausage*. These healthy dishes add up to a meal so totally satisfying, you'll want to repeat the celebration frequently.

Menu

Mulled Citrus Cider

Corn-Oat Waffles with
Strawberry-Apricot Sauce

Turkey-Apple Sausage

33

Weekend Brunch

Menu

Mulled Citrus Cider
Corn-Oat Waffles with Strawberry-
    Apricot Sauce
Turkey-Apple Sausage
    (see recipe, page 36)

Menu Countdown

1 Day Ahead: Prepare and refrigerate
the batter for the *Corn-Oat Waffles.*
30 Minutes Ahead: Mix and shape the
Turkey-Apple Sausage. Refrigerate until
ready to cook.

20 Minutes Ahead: Prepare the
Strawberry-Apricot Sauce; cover
the saucepan to keep warm.
15 Minutes Ahead: Preheat the broiler
and the waffle iron. Mix the *Mulled Citrus
Cider.* Let simmer while you cook the
sausage and waffles.
10 Minutes Ahead: Start cooking the
sausage and baking the waffles. As each
waffle finishes baking, place on a paper-
towel-lined baking sheet.
To Serve: Pat sausage with paper towels
to remove fat.

Mulled Citrus Cider

0 g fat
0 mg cholesterol

*Keep a batch of this spicy cider in your refrigerator up to four days. Then, heat up a cupful in
a small saucepan or your microwave oven. (Pictured on pages 32–33.)*

2¼ **cups apple cider *or* juice**
  ¾ **cup orange juice**
   3 **inches stick cinnamon, broken**
      Dash ground cloves

● In a large saucepan combine apple cider or
juice, orange juice, stick cinnamon, and cloves.
Bring to boiling; reduce heat. Simmer, covered,
for 10 minutes. Remove stick cinnamon.

   4 **cinnamon sticks (optional)**

● Ladle into 4 mugs. Garnish with cinnamon
sticks, if desired. Makes 4 (6-ounce) servings.

Nutrition information per serving: 89 calories, 0 g saturated fat,
0 g monounsaturated fat, 0 g polyunsaturated fat, 0 g protein,
22 g carbohydrate, 4 mg sodium, 272 mg potassium.

Corn-Oat Waffles

16 g fat
2 mg cholesterol

Make the batter the night before and save a step the morning of your brunch. Since the leavening is yeast, the waffles rise overnight in the refrigerator. (Pictured on pages 32–33.)

1¼ cups all-purpose flour
  1 cup yellow cornmeal
 ½ cup oat bran
  3 tablespoons sugar
  1 package active dry yeast
 ½ teaspoon salt

● In a large mixing bowl combine flour, cornmeal, oat bran, sugar, yeast, and salt.

  2 cups skim milk
  4 egg whites
 ¼ cup cooking oil

● Add milk, egg whites, and cooking oil. Beat with a rotary beater or an electric mixer on medium speed about 1 minute or till thoroughly combined. Cover bowl loosely. Chill for 2 to 24 hours. *Or,* let stand at room temperature about 1 hour or till the mixture is bubbly and slightly thickened.

Nonstick spray coating
Strawberry-Apricot Sauce

● To bake, stir batter. Spray a *cold* waffle iron with nonstick coating. Heat waffle iron. Pour batter into waffle iron. (Check manufacturer's directions for amount of batter to use.) Close lid quickly; do not open during baking.

  Bake according to the manufacturer's directions. Use a fork to remove the baked waffle from the waffle iron. Keep warm. Repeat with remaining batter. Serve with Strawberry-Apricot Sauce. Makes 4 servings.

Nutrition information per serving: 675 calories, 2 g saturated fat, 4 g monounsaturated fat, 9 g polyunsaturated fat, 18 g protein, 121 g carbohydrate, 391 mg sodium, 695 mg potassium.

Strawberry-Apricot Sauce
1 16-ounce can unpeeled apricot
   halves, drained
2 tablespoons sugar
1 tablespoon cornstarch
1 cup apricot nectar
1 cup sliced strawberries

Cut apricot halves in half; set aside. In a medium saucepan combine sugar and cornstarch. Stir in apricot nectar. Cook and stir over medium heat till mixture is thickened and bubbly. Cook and stir for 2 minutes more. Gently stir in strawberries and apricots. Heat through. Serve warm.

Turkey-Apple Sausage

1 g fat
36 mg cholesterol

In purchased sausage, up to 80 percent of the calories come from fat. In our sausage, made with turkey breast, only 12 percent of the calories come from fat. (Pictured on pages 32–33.)

1 slightly beaten egg white
¼ cup soft bread crumbs
¼ cup finely chopped peeled apple
¼ teaspoon salt
¼ teaspoon ground sage
⅛ teaspoon pepper
½ pound ground raw turkey breast
   (see tip, below), lean ground raw
   turkey, *or* lean ground beef

● In a medium mixing bowl combine egg white, bread crumbs, apple, salt, sage, and pepper. Add ground turkey or beef; mix well. Shape into eight small patties, about 2½ inches in diameter.

Apple slices (optional)
Fresh sage leaves (optional)

● Place sausage patties on the unheated rack of a broiler pan. Broil 4 to 5 inches from the heat for 4 minutes. Turn and broil for 4 to 5 minutes more or till no longer pink. Pat sausage patties with paper towels. Arrange on a serving plate. Garnish with apple slices and fresh sage leaves, if desired. Makes 4 servings.

Nutrition information per serving: 73 calories, 0 g saturated fat, 0 g monounsaturated fat, 0 g polyunsaturated fat, 14 g protein, 3 g carbohydrate, 182 mg sodium, 148 mg potassium.

Spiced Turkey-Apple Sausage
½ teaspoon ground cinnamon
¼ teaspoon ground ginger

Prepare Turkey-Apple Sausage as above, *except* omit sage and pepper. Add cinnamon and ginger to the egg white mixture.

Nutrition information per serving: 73 calories, 1 g total fat (0 g saturated fat, 0 g monounsaturated fat, 0 g polyunsaturated fat), 36 mg cholesterol, 14 g protein, 3 g carbohydrate, 182 mg sodium, 148 mg potassium.

Buying Ground Turkey

It pays to take a second look at the label when buying ground turkey. Choose turkey that's at least 90 percent lean by weight. If there's no label, take a look at the meat. A lot of little white specks indicates that fat and skin were ground up with the turkey meat. In some areas you can purchase ground turkey breast, which generally is leaner than other ground turkey.

To assure that you have the leanest ground turkey, grind your own. Start with a turkey breast. (Avoid the self-basting kind, because they're frequently injected with saturated fat.) Remove the skin and discard it. Grind the meat in a food grinder using a coarse blade. Package the meat in ½- or 1-pound packages and freeze till you're ready to use them.

Vegetarian Pasta Dinner

Here's the cast of recipes for a smashingly sumptuous meatless dinner. Ample servings of *Cheese Manicotti* take center stage. Tofu and low-fat ricotta and mozzarella cheeses keep the fat down, with no sacrifice of either flavor or protein. *Marinated Vegetables* co-stars as a crisp, cool accompaniment to the hearty pasta casserole. For the final act, *Crunchy Fruit Bake* enters. Choose either a blueberry or peach filling for this cereal-topped fruit crisp. On with the show!

Menu

Cheese Manicotti *(see recipe, page 38)*
Marinated Vegetables
Crunchy Fruit Bake with Whipped
   Topping *(see recipes, page 39)*

Menu Countdown

4 Hours to 1 Day Ahead: Make the *Marinated Vegetables.*
1¼ Hours Ahead: Prepare the fruit filling for the *Crunchy Fruit Bake.*
1 Hour Ahead: Cook and drain the manicotti shells. Prepare the filling and assemble *Cheese Manicotti.*
55 Minutes Ahead: Preheat the oven.
45 Minutes Ahead: Bake the *Crunchy Fruit Bake.*
30 Minutes Ahead: Add the *Cheese Manicotti* to the oven.
10 Minutes Ahead: Assemble the ingredients for the *Whipped Topping.* (Whip the topping just before serving the *Crunchy Fruit Bake.*)

Marinated Vegetables

1 g fat
1 mg cholesterol

Reduced-calorie salad dressings vary in the amount of fat they contain. Some are oil-free, but others contain some oil. Compare the labels of several brands to find the one lowest in fat.

2 **cups cut fresh green beans *or* one 9-ounce package frozen cut green beans *or* frozen Italian-style beans**
1 **cup fresh *or* frozen cauliflower flowerets**

● Cook fresh green beans and cauliflower in a small amount of boiling water for 8 to 10 minutes or till crisp-tender. (Or, cook frozen green beans and cauliflower according to package directions, *except* omit salt.) Drain vegetables. Place in a mixing bowl.

¼ **cup reduced-calorie *or* oil-free Italian salad dressing**
1 **2-ounce jar sliced pimiento, drained**

● Add salad dressing and pimiento. Toss till vegetables are coated. Cover and chill for 4 to 24 hours. Makes 4 servings.

Nutrition information per serving: 41 calories, 0 g saturated fat, 0 g monounsaturated fat, 0 g polyunsaturated fat, 2 g protein, 8 g carbohydrate, 122 mg sodium, 289 mg potassium.

Cheese Manicotti

9 g fat
17 mg cholesterol

Three cheeses, tofu, and pasta team up to provide plenty of protein in this robust casserole.

8 ounces tofu (bean curd), drained
2 egg whites
½ cup low-fat *or* part-skim ricotta cheese
¼ cup grated romano *or* Parmesan cheese
1 tablespoon snipped parsley
½ teaspoon salt
⅛ teaspoon pepper

● For cheese filling, pat tofu dry with paper towels. In a medium mixing bowl mash tofu with a fork. Lightly beat eggs whites with a fork. Stir egg whites, ricotta cheese, romano or Parmesan cheese, parsley, salt, and pepper into tofu.

8 manicotti shells, cooked and drained

● Spoon about *3 tablespoons* of the cheese filling into *each* manicotti shell. Arrange filled shells in a 13x9x2-inch baking dish.

1 16-ounce can tomatoes, cut up
1 8-ounce can tomato sauce
2 teaspoons dried basil, crushed
1 teaspoon sugar
¼ teaspoon garlic powder

● In another mixing bowl stir together *undrained* tomatoes, tomato sauce, basil, sugar, and garlic powder. Pour tomato mixture over shells in the baking dish.

¼ cup shredded part-skim mozzarella cheese (1 ounce)

● Bake in a 350° oven for 25 to 30 minutes or till heated through. Sprinkle with mozzarella cheese. Let stand 5 minutes before serving. Makes 4 servings.

Nutrition information per serving: 269 calories, 4 g saturated fat, 2 g monounsaturated fat, 2 g polyunsaturated fat, 19 g protein, 31 g carbohydrate, 989 mg sodium, 634 mg potassium.

Cut off an 8-ounce piece of tofu. (Place the remaining tofu and liquid from the package in an airtight container. Save for another use.) Pat the tofu piece dry with paper towels and place in a bowl. To mash the tofu, press down with a dinner fork and break it up into tiny pieces.

Crunchy Fruit Bake

3 g fat
0 mg cholesterol

Shredded wheat cereal sweetened with brown sugar makes a yummy topping for this fruit crisp.

3 **cups fresh *or* frozen unsweetened blueberries *and/or* sliced, peeled peaches**
2 **tablespoons brown sugar**
2 **teaspoons cornstarch**
¼ **teaspoon ground cinnamon**

● In a mixing bowl toss together fruit, brown sugar, cornstarch, and cinnamon. Transfer mixture to a 1-quart casserole. Cover and bake in a 350° oven for 20 minutes. Stir fruit.

½ **cup bite-size shredded wheat biscuits**
2 **tablespoons brown sugar**
1 **tablespoon margarine, melted**
Whipped Topping (optional)

● Meanwhile, for crumb topping, put the shredded wheat biscuits in a plastic bag. Use your hands or a rolling pin to coarsely crush the cereal. Stir together cereal crumbs, brown sugar, and margarine.

Sprinkle the crumb topping over the fruit mixture. Bake, uncovered, for 20 to 25 minutes more or till the mixture is bubbly around the edges. Cool slightly. Serve with Whipped Topping, if desired. Makes 4 servings.

Nutrition information per serving: 163 calories, 1 g saturated fat, 1 g monounsaturated fat, 1 g polyunsaturated fat, 1 g protein, 34 g carbohydrate, 47 mg sodium, 165 mg potassium.

Whipped Topping

0 g fat
1 mg cholesterol

Look at the savings! An equal-size serving of whipped cream would contain 12 g of fat.

¼ **cup ice water**
1 **tablespoon lemon juice**
½ **teaspoon vanilla**
⅓ **cup nonfat dry milk powder**

● In a small mixing bowl combine water, lemon juice, and vanilla. Stir in nonfat dry milk powder. Beat with an electric mixer on high speed for 3 to 6 minutes or till soft peaks form.

2 **tablespoons sugar**

● Add sugar. Beat for 1 minute more. Serve immediately. Makes 6 (¼-cup) servings.

Note: If desired, freeze any leftover topping or prepare the topping ahead of time and store in the freezer. To freeze, dollop topping on a waxed-paper-lined baking sheet. Freeze till firm. Transfer to an airtight container or plastic bag.

To serve, remove the number of dollops you need. Let stand at room temperature for 10 to 15 minutes or in the refrigerator about 1 hour.

Nutrition information per serving: 30 calories, 0 g saturated fat, 0 g monounsaturated fat, 0 g polyunsaturated fat, 1 g protein, 6 g carbohydrate, 21 mg sodium, 67 mg potassium.

Soup and Salad Supper

Spicy *Chicken-Barley Soup* and crisp, cold *Garden Salad* make a contrasting, yet tasty, pair in this supper. Stewed tomatoes and bottled hot pepper sauce flavor the soup, and a cool and creamy honey-yogurt dressing tops fresh greens in the salad. Slice some crusty French bread and add some refreshing melon to complete this flavor-packed meal.

Menu

Chicken-Barley Soup

Garden Salad

French bread

Melon wedge

Soup and Salad Supper

Menu

Chicken-Barley Soup
Garden Salad
French bread
Melon wedge

Menu Countdown

1 Day Ahead: Cook the chicken for the *Chicken-Barley Soup.* Refrigerate the chicken and the broth.

1 Hour Ahead: Prepare dressing for *Garden Salad.* Chill till serving time.
45 Minutes Ahead: Finish preparing *Chicken-Barley Soup.*
20 Minutes Ahead: Preheat oven to 300° to warm French bread.
15 Minutes Ahead: Prepare the salad ingredients while the soup simmers.
10 Minutes Ahead: Heat French bread in oven about 5 minutes. Cut up the melon; refrigerate.
5 Minutes Ahead: Slice the French bread. Add dressing to salad.

Garden Salad

3 g fat
2 mg cholesterol

Crumbled Melba toast makes a low-fat substitute for croutons in this fresh-tasting salad. (Pictured on pages 40–41.)

⅓ **cup plain low-fat yogurt**
¼ **cup chopped, cucumber**
1 **tablespoon reduced-calorie mayonnaise *or* salad dressing**
1 **tablespoon snipped chives *or* sliced green onion**
1½ **teaspoons snipped fresh dill *or* ½ teaspoon dried dillweed**
¼ **teaspoon seasoned salt**

● For dressing, in a small mixing bowl stir together yogurt, cucumber, mayonnaise or salad dressing, chives or green onion, dill, and seasoned salt. Mix well.

4 **cups torn salad greens**
1 **large green *or* sweet red pepper, coarsely chopped**
½ **cup sliced radishes**
10 **Melba toast rounds, broken into small pieces**

● In a salad bowl arrange greens, green or red pepper, and radishes. Toss to mix. Add dressing. Toss till greens are coated. Sprinkle with Melba toast pieces. Makes 4 servings.

Nutrition information per serving: 91 calories, 1 g saturated fat, 0 g monounsaturated fat, 1 g polyunsaturated fat, 4 g protein, 15 g carbohydrate, 290 mg sodium, 255 mg potassium.

Chicken-Barley Soup

6 g fat
70 mg cholesterol

Chilling the broth overnight is essential for removing all the fat. (Pictured on pages 40–41.)

1½ **pounds meaty chicken pieces**
3 **cups water**
1 **large onion, chopped (1 cup)**
1 **bay leaf**
1 **teaspoon salt**
¼ **teaspoon pepper**

● Remove the skin from chicken pieces; discard skin. Place chicken in a 4-quart oven. Add water, onion, bay leaf, salt, and pepper. Bring to boiling; reduce heat. Simmer, covered, for 40 to 50 minutes or till chicken is tender.

● Remove chicken pieces. Strain broth. Cover and chill chicken and broth for 6 to 24 hours or till the fat in broth solidifies. Use a large spoon to lift the solid fat from the broth.

   Remove bones from chicken. Discard bones. Coarsely chop chicken. Set the chicken aside. Measure broth. If necessary, add water to make 3 cups.

1 **16-ounce can tomatoes, cut up**
1 **8-ounce can tomato sauce**
1 **cup frozen crinkle-cut carrots**
1 **cup frozen cut green beans**
⅓ **cup quick-cooking barley**
1 **teaspoon dried savory, crushed**
   Several dashes bottled hot
      pepper sauce

● In the Dutch oven combine the 3 cups of broth, *undrained* tomatoes, tomato sauce, carrots, beans, barley, savory, and hot pepper sauce. Bring to boiling; reduce heat. Simmer, covered, about 10 minutes or till barley and vegetables are tender. Stir in chicken; heat through. Discard bay leaf. Makes 4 servings.

Nutrition information per serving: 286 calories, 2 g saturated fat, 2 g monounsaturated fat, 2 g polyunsaturated fat, 28 g protein, 31 g carbohydrate, 1,149 mg sodium, 850 mg potassium.

Make-Ahead Dinner

When you know you'll be on the go all day, find some time to cook ahead. This time schedule allows a lot of flexibility because all the dishes can be prepared up to 24 hours before the meal.

** Chicken-Bulgur Salad is a no-cook main dish that goes together in minutes and waits for you in the refrigerator. If you like, make the crispy Rye Breadsticks several days ahead and freeze them. For dessert, pick up an angel cake at your bakery or grocery store.**

Menu

Chicken-Bulgur Salad
Rye Breadsticks
Angel cake

Menu Countdown

At least 4 Hours Ahead: Mix and knead the dough for the *Rye Breadsticks.* Let rise.
At least 3½ Hours Ahead: Make the *Chicken-Bulgur Salad.* Chill till serving time.
At least 2½ Hours Ahead: Finish making the breadsticks.
Just Before Serving: Rinse the lettuce for the salad; dry. Add the tomato to the bulgur mixture. Arrange lettuce, chicken slices, and bulgur mixture on individual serving plates.

Chicken-Bulgur Salad

4 g fat
51 mg cholesterol

Tangy apricots and sweet raisins flavor this tasty one-dish meal.

½	**cup bulgur**
1	**8-ounce carton plain low-fat yogurt**
¼	**cup snipped dried apricots**
¼	**cup snipped parsley**
¼	**cup sliced green onions**
¼	**cup raisins**
¼	**cup orange juice**
½	**teaspoon salt**
½	**teaspoon dried oregano, crushed**

● Rinse and drain bulgur. In a medium mixing bowl stir together bulgur, yogurt, apricots, parsley, green onions, raisins, orange juice, salt, and oregano. Cover and chill for 3 to 24 hours.

1	**large tomato, seeded and chopped**
	Lettuce leaves
8	**ounces sliced cooked chicken breast** *or* **turkey breast**

● Add tomato to bulgur mixture. Stir gently. Line 4 plates with lettuce leaves. Arrange chicken or turkey slices on lettuce. Spoon bulgur mixture on top. Makes 4 servings.

Nutrition information per serving: 276 calories, 1 g saturated fat, 1 g monounsaturated fat, 1 g polyunsaturated fat, 24 g protein, 37 g carbohydrate, 360 mg sodium, 684 mg potassium.

Rye Breadsticks

1 g fat
0 mg cholesterol

For crisper breadsticks, turn off the oven after baking is complete, but leave the breadsticks in the oven for 15 minutes more.

1¼ to 1¾ cups all-purpose flour
1 package active dry yeast
½ teaspoon salt
1 cup warm water (120° to 130°)
1 tablespoon cooking oil
¾ cup rye *or* whole wheat flour
¼ cup toasted wheat germ *or* cornmeal
2 tablespoons snipped parsley

● In a small mixing bowl combine *1 cup* of the all-purpose flour, yeast, and salt. Stir in water and cooking oil. Beat with an electric mixer on low to medium speed for 30 seconds, scraping the bowl. Beat on high speed for 3 minutes.

Using a spoon, stir in rye or whole wheat flour, wheat germ or cornmeal, and parsley. Stir in as much of the remaining all-purpose flour as you can.

● Turn dough out onto a lightly floured surface. Knead in enough remaining all-purpose flour to make a moderately stiff dough that is smooth and elastic (6 to 8 minutes total). Place in a lightly greased bowl; turn once to grease surface. Cover; let rise in a warm place till double (about 1 hour).

Nonstick spray coating
1 slightly beaten egg white
1 tablespoon water
2 tablespoons snipped parsley (optional)

● Punch dough down. Turn out onto a lightly floured surface. Divide dough into 4 portions. Cover; let rest for 10 minutes.

Meanwhile, spray a large baking sheet with nonstick coating. Divide each dough portion into 6 pieces. Roll each piece into an 8-inch rope. Place on baking sheet. Cover; let rise in a warm place till nearly double (about 30 minutes). Mix together egg white and water. Brush over breadsticks. Sprinkle with parsley, if desired. Bake in a 375° oven about 15 minutes or till light brown. Transfer to a wire rack. Cool completely. Store breadsticks in an airtight container. Makes 24.

Note: To save time, substitute 1 package *quick-rise active dry yeast* for the active dry yeast. After kneading the dough, cover and let rest for 10 minutes (omit the first rising). Shape as directed. Cover; let rise till nearly double (20 to 25 minutes).

Nutrition information per breadstick: 48 calories, 0 g saturated fat, 0 g monounsaturated fat, 0 g polyunsaturated fat, 2 g protein, 8 g carbohydrate, 50 mg sodium, 38 mg potassium.

Stir-Fry Dinner

Perfectly suited for a low-fat meal, stir-fries take little fat to cook and sport lots of vegetables. Plus, they're amazingly fast. So bring out your wok or skillet and start experimenting with stir-fry foods.

Menu

Easy Oriental Soup

Gingered Pork *or*
Chicken Stir-Fry

Tossed salad

Rolls

Berry-Sauced Ice Milk

Stir-Fry Dinner

Menu

Easy Oriental Soup
Gingered Pork *or* Chicken Stir-Fry
  (see recipe, page 50)
Tossed salad
Rolls
Berry-Sauced Ice Milk
  (see recipe, page 50)

Menu Countdown

1¼ Hours Ahead: If using pork, place it in the freezer to partially freeze.

55 Minutes Ahead: Prepare sauce and cantaloupe for *Berry-Sauced Ice Milk.* Set the table.
45 Minutes Ahead: Slice vegetables for stir-fry and *Easy Oriental Soup.* Make a tossed salad.
30 Minutes Ahead: Mix sauce for the stir-fry. Slice the frozen pork or the chicken. Begin cooking rice.
20 Minutes Ahead: Prepare *Easy Oriental Soup.* Cover to keep warm.
15 Minutes Ahead: Begin cooking the stir-fry.
To serve: Transfer stir-fry to a serving platter; cover to keep warm. Arrange rolls in a basket. Ladle soup into bowls.

Easy Oriental Soup

2 g fat
12 mg cholesterol

Red pepper gives this appetizer just the right kick. (Pictured on pages 46–47.)

2 14½-ounce cans chicken broth
1 cup sliced fresh mushrooms
2 green onions, sliced
¼ teaspoon garlic powder
⅛ teaspoon ground red pepper

● In a medium saucepan combine chicken broth, mushrooms, green onions, garlic powder, and ground red pepper. Bring to boiling.

½ cup fine noodles (1 ounce)

● Break noodles slightly and add to the boiling broth mixture. Reduce heat. Simmer soup, uncovered, about 5 minutes or till noodles and mushrooms are tender. Ladle into 4 small soup bowls. Makes 4 servings.

Nutrition information per serving: 66 calories, 0 g saturated fat, 0 g polyunsaturated fat, 1 g monounsaturated fat, 6 g protein, 7 g carbohydrate, 658 mg sodium, 272 mg potassium.

Gingered Pork

9 g fat
58 mg cholesterol

Relish the classic combo of apple and pork in this tasty stir-fry. (Pictured on pages 46–47.)

12 ounces lean boneless pork **½ cup apple juice** **3 tablespoons soy sauce *or* sodium-** **reduced soy sauce** **1 tablespoon cornstarch**	● Trim fat from pork. Partially freeze pork. Cut across the grain into thin bite-size strips. For sauce, in a small bowl stir together the juice, soy sauce, and cornstarch. Set aside.

Nonstick spray coating **2 teaspoons grated gingerroot** **2 cups cauliflower flowerets (about** **½ of a medium head)** **1 medium zucchini, sliced** **1 small onion, cut into thin wedges**	● Spray a *cold* wok or large skillet with nonstick coating. Preheat over medium-high heat till a drop of water sizzles. Add gingerroot; stir-fry for 15 seconds. Add cauliflower; stir-fry for 2 minutes. Add zucchini and onion; stir-fry for 2 to 3 minutes more or till vegetables are crisp-tender. Remove vegetables. Add pork. Stir-fry about 3 minutes or till pork is no longer pink. Push pork from center of the wok or skillet.

2 cups hot cooked rice **Sweet red pepper rings (optional)**	● Stir sauce. Add sauce to the center of the wok or skillet. Cook and stir till thickened and bubbly. Cook and stir for 1 minute more. Return vegetables to wok or skillet. Stir to coat with sauce. Heat through. Serve over hot rice. Garnish with sweet red pepper rings, if desired. Makes 4 servings.

Nutrition information per serving: 320 calories, 3 g saturated fat, 1 g polyunsaturated fat, 4 g monounsaturated fat, 22 g protein, 36 g carbohydrate, 825 mg sodium, 649 mg potassium.

Holding a sharp knife at a 45-degree angle, slice the pork across the grain into thin pieces for stir-frying. You'll find it easier to cut very thin pieces if the meat has been partially frozen (allow about 45 minutes to partially freeze).

Berry-Sauced Ice Milk

2 g fat
6 mg cholesterol

Complete a spicy dinner with this cool, refreshing dessert. (Pictured on pages 46–47.)

2 tablespoons sugar
1½ teaspoons cornstarch
½ cup orange juice
½ cup fresh *or* frozen blueberries

● For sauce, in a small saucepan stir together sugar and cornstarch. Add orange juice and berries. Cook and stir over medium heat till thickened and bubbly. Cook and stir for 2 minutes more. Cool to room temperature.

1⅓ cups vanilla ice milk *or* frozen vanilla yogurt
½ of a small cantaloupe, thinly sliced and peeled

● Place a ⅓-*cup* scoop of ice milk in *each* of 4 dessert bowls. Arrange cantaloupe around ice milk. Spoon sauce over ice milk. Serves 4.

Nutrition information per serving: 135 calories, 1 g saturated fat, 0 g polyunsaturated fat, 1 g monounsaturated fat, 3 g protein, 28 g carbohydrate, 42 mg sodium, 371 mg potassium.

Chicken Stir-Fry

8 g fat
64 mg cholesterol

3 tablespoons soy sauce
2 teaspoons cornstarch
1 teaspoon sugar
1 teaspoon rice vinegar *or* white wine vinegar
½ teaspoon instant chicken bouillon granules
1 pound boned skinless chicken breast halves *or* turkey breast tenderloin steaks

● For sauce, in a small bowl stir together soy sauce, cornstarch, sugar, vinegar, bouillon granules, and ⅓ cup *water*. Set aside.
  Rinse the chicken or turkey and pat dry. Cut into thin bite-size strips. Set aside.

Nonstick spray coating
1 teaspoon grated gingerroot
2 cups sliced fresh mushrooms
1 6-ounce package frozen pea pods, thawed, *or* 1½ cups fresh pea pods
1 tablespoon cooking oil

● Spray a *cold* wok or large skillet with nonstick coating. Preheat wok or skillet over medium-high heat. Add gingerroot and stir-fry 15 seconds. Add fresh mushrooms. Stir-fry for 1 minute. Add pea pods. Stir-fry 1 to 2 minutes more. Remove vegetables from wok.
  Add oil to wok, if necessary. Add *half* of the chicken to wok. Stir-fry 2 to 3 minutes or till no longer pink. Remove from wok. Repeat with remaining chicken. Return all chicken to wok.

1 8½-ounce can bamboo shoots, drained
2 cups hot cooked rice

● Push chicken from center of wok. Stir sauce; add to center of wok. Cook and stir till thickened and bubbly. Add vegetables and bamboo shoots. Cook and stir till heated through. Serve over hot rice. Makes 4 servings.

Nutrition information per serving: 336 calories, 1 g saturated fat, 3 g polyunsaturated fat, 2 g monounsaturated fat, 30 g protein, 36 g carbohydrate, 948 mg sodium, 526 mg potassium.

Foods to Love, Foods to Avoid

You probably have a fairly good idea of the foods that are good and bad for a low-fat diet. However, there may be a few surprises in store as you read this list of low-fat and high-fat foods. For more specific details, check the charts on pages 119–124.

Foods to Love

Lean Meat, Poultry, and Fish:
Beef *(round, sirloin, chuck, loin, ground)*
Veal *(except ground)*
Pork *(loin, leg, ham)*
Lamb *(leg, loin, arm)*
Chicken *(no skin)*
Turkey *(no skin)*
Fish
Dried peas and beans *(lentils, kidney beans, navy beans, black-eyed peas, tofu)*
Egg whites

Fruits and Vegetables:
Most fresh, frozen, and canned fruits and vegetables

Dairy Products:
Skim milk
Low-fat buttermilk
Evaporated skim milk
Low-fat yogurt
Low-fat cheeses *(cottage, farmers, pot, sapsago)*

Breads and Cereals:
Rice
Pasta
Pita bread

Bagels
English muffins
Graham crackers
Corn tortillas
Melba toast
Pancakes
Whole-grain bread
Cereal *(oats, farina)*
Low-fat crackers, breadsticks, pretzels

Miscellaneous:
Nonstick spray coating
Mustard
Fig bars
Angel cake
Tapioca pudding

Foods to Avoid

Meat, Poultry, Fish:
Beef *(corned beef, brisket rib eye, ribs)*
organ meats *(liver, kidney)**
Pork *(frankfurters, luncheon meats, sausages, spare ribs, bacon)*
Shrimp*, crab*, oysters*
Goose and duck
Egg yolks*
Nuts

Fruits and Vegetables:
Avocado
Olives
Coconut

Dairy Products:
Butter
Cheese
Whole and 2% milk
Cream
Creamed cottage cheese
Cream cheese
Ice cream

Breads and Cereals:
Egg noodles*
Chow mein noodles
Granola
Purchased bakery products *(muffins, cookies, cakes)*
Flour tortillas
Biscuits
Croissants
Butter rolls

Sweet rolls, Danish pastries, doughnuts
Waffles

Miscellaneous:
Chocolate
Lard
Hydrogenated shortening
Coconut, palm, and palm kernel oil
Butter
Nondairy creamers
Potato chips

*Foods high in cholesterol.

Foods to Use in Moderation

Lobster
Clams
Mussels
Salmon
Herring
Part-skim mozzarella cheese
1% milk

Parmesan cheese
Ice milk
Sherbet, Frozen yogurt
Polyunsaturated and monounsaturated oil
Hard candies and jelly beans

Main Dishes

Selecting the main dish for a low-fat meal can present quite a challenge. But you'll find lots to choose from in this amazing assortment of fat-trimmed entrées. Your options range from homey Hamburger Pie to new-fashioned Lemon-Fennel Fish. In each recipe, we start with lean poultry, fish, beef, or pork. And, we keep them lean with cooking techniques and ingredients that add lots of flavor but little fat.

Chicken Parmigiano

6 g fat
75 mg cholesterol

Try a super-fast version of a classic.

¼ cup fine dry bread crumbs 2 tablespoons grated Parmesan cheese	● In a pie plate or on a sheet of waxed paper, combine bread crumbs and Parmesan cheese.
2 whole medium chicken breasts (about 1½ pounds total), skinned, boned, and halved lengthwise, *or* 4 turkey breast tenderloin steaks (about 12 ounces total) 2 tablespoons skim milk Nonstick spray coating	● Rinse chicken; pat dry. Brush chicken with milk. Coat with crumb mixture. Spray a *cold* large skillet with nonstick coating. Preheat skillet, then add chicken. Cook over medium heat for 8 to 10 minutes or till tender and no longer pink, turning the pieces occasionally to brown evenly. Transfer to a platter; cover to keep warm. Wipe skillet with paper towels.
1 14½-ounce can stewed tomatoes 2 teaspoons cornstarch ½ teaspoon dried Italian seasoning	● In the same skillet combine tomatoes, cornstarch, and Italian seasoning. Cook and stir till thickened and bubbly. Cook and stir for 2 minutes more.
1 tablespoon grated Parmesan cheese	● Spoon tomato mixture over chicken. Sprinkle with Parmesan cheese. Serves 4.

Nutrition information per serving: 227 calories, 2 g saturated fat, 2 g monounsaturated fat, 1 g polyunsaturated fat, 30 g protein, 13 g carbohydrate, 463 mg sodium, 241 mg potassium.

Thyme-Mustard Chicken

5 g fat
72 mg cholesterol

¼ cup toasted wheat germ 3 tablespoons fine dry bread crumbs ¾ teaspoon dried thyme, crushed	● In a pie plate or on a sheet of waxed paper, combine wheat germ, bread crumbs, thyme, and ¼ teaspoon *salt*.
1 tablespoon Dijon-style mustard 1 tablespoon water	● In a small bowl stir together Dijon mustard and water.
2 whole medium chicken breasts (about 1½ pounds total), skinned, boned, and halved lengthwise, *or* 4 turkey breast tenderloin steaks (about 12 ounces total) Nonstick spray coating Lemon slices (optional) Dijon-style mustard (optional)	● Rinse chicken; pat dry. Brush chicken with mustard mixture; roll in crumb mixture. Spray a *cold* large skillet with nonstick coating. Preheat skillet, then add chicken. Cook over medium heat for 8 to 10 minutes or till tender and no longer pink, turning the pieces occasionally to brown evenly. Serve with lemon slices and Dijon mustard, if desired. Serves 4.

Nutrition information per serving: 197 calories, 1 g saturated fat, 2 g monounsaturated fat, 1 g polyunsaturated fat, 29 g protein, 7 g carbohydrate, 283 mg sodium, 289 mg potassium.

Turkey Chili

12 g fat
71 mg cholesterol

Nonstick spray coating
1 pound lean ground raw turkey
1 cup chopped celery

● Spray a *cold* large skillet with nonstick coating. Add turkey and celery. Cook till turkey is no longer pink, stirring to break up pieces.

1 16-ounce can tomatoes, cut up
1 16-ounce can red kidney beans, drained
1 8-ounce can tomato sauce
1 6-ounce can vegetable juice cocktail
1 bay leaf
2 tablespoons dried minced onion
1 teaspoon dried basil, crushed
½ teaspoon instant beef bouillon granules
½ teaspoon ground cumin
¼ teaspoon garlic powder
¼ teaspoon crushed red pepper (optional)
Toasted Pita Chips (optional)

● Stir in tomatoes; beans; tomato sauce; juice cocktail; bay leaf; onion; basil; bouillon granules; cumin; garlic powder; red pepper, if desired; and ½ cup *water*. Bring to boiling; reduce heat. Simmer, uncovered, for 20 minutes, stirring occasionally. Discard bay leaf.
   Serve with Toasted Pita Chips, if desired. Makes 4 servings.

Nutrition information per serving: 380 calories, 4 g saturated fat, 5 g monounsaturated fat, 3 g polyunsaturated fat, 33 g protein, 36 g carbohydrate, 926 mg sodium, 1,272 mg potassium.

 Microwave Directions: In a 3-quart microwave-safe casserole cook turkey and celery, uncovered, on 100% power (high) 5 to 7 minutes or till no pink remains, stirring to break up pieces. Stir in tomatoes; beans;

tomato sauce; juice cocktail; bay leaf; onion; basil; bouillon granules; cumin; garlic; red pepper, if desired; and ½ cup *water*. Cook, covered, on high for 7 to 9 minutes or till desired consistency. Continue as above.

Toasted Pita Chips
4 pita bread rounds

Split each pita horizontally in half. Cut each half into 6 wedges. Spread in a single layer on a baking sheet. Bake in a 350° oven about 10 minutes or till crisp. Serve warm. Serves 4.

Nutrition information per serving: 165 calories, 0 g total fat (0 g saturated fat, 0 g polyunsaturated fat, 0 g monounsaturated fat), 0 mg cholesterol, 6 g protein, 33 g carbohydrate, 339 mg sodium, 71 mg potassium.

Attention: Microwave Owners

Recipes in this book with microwave directions were tested in countertop microwave ovens rated at 600 to 700 watts. Times are approximate because microwave ovens vary by manufacturer. The best rule for micro-cooking is to check the food at the end of the minimum cooking time. Then, add more time as needed to achieve the desired doneness.

**Toasted
Pita Chips**

Turkey Chili

Chinese Chicken Salad

6 g fat
62 mg cholesterol

A touch of sesame oil lends a nutty flavor to the dressing.

1 cup finely chopped cooked chicken
 ***or* turkey**
½ cup fresh *or* canned bean sprouts
¼ cup chopped water chestnuts
1 green onion, thinly sliced

● In a medium bowl combine chopped chicken, bean sprouts, water chestnuts, and green onion. Set aside.

4 teaspoons soy sauce
1 tablespoon white wine vinegar
½ teaspoon sesame oil
⅛ teaspoon pepper

● In a custard cup stir together soy sauce, vinegar, sesame oil, and pepper. Pour over chicken mixture. Toss well. Cover and chill.

2 large tomatoes
 Lettuce leaves

● To serve, cut out ½ inch of the core from each tomato. Invert tomatoes. Cut each tomato from top to, but not quite through, stem end, making 6 wedges. Spread wedges slightly apart. Fill tomatoes with chilled chicken mixture. Serve on lettuce leaves. Makes 2 servings.

Nutrition information per serving: 193 calories, 2 g saturated fat, 2 g monounsaturated fat, 2 g polyunsaturated fat, 23 g protein, 11 g carbohydrate, 761 mg sodium, 554 mg potassium.

Orange-Mint Chicken

3 g fat
65 mg cholesterol

Tastes equally delicious using marjoram or chervil instead of the mint.

2 whole medium chicken breasts
 (about 1½ pounds total), skinned
 and halved lengthwise
 Salt (optional)
 Pepper (optional)

● Rinse chicken; pat dry. Place chicken, bone side up, on the unheated rack of a broiler pan. Season with salt and pepper, if desired. Broil 4 to 5 inches from the heat for 15 minutes.

⅓ cup orange marmalade
1 tablespoon lemon juice
½ teaspoon dried mint, crushed

● Meanwhile, for glaze, in a small saucepan combine marmalade, juice, and mint. Cook and stir over low heat till well blended.
  Brush some of the glaze over bone side of chicken; turn chicken over. Continue broiling for 10 to 15 minutes or till tender and no longer pink, brushing with glaze several times during the last few minutes. Serve any remaining glaze over chicken. Makes 4 servings.

Nutrition information per serving: 196 calories, 1 g saturated fat, 1 g monounsaturated fat, 1 g polyunsaturated fat, 24 g protein, 19 g carbohydrate, 94 mg sodium, 363 mg potassium.

Honey-Mustard Chicken

3 g fat
65 mg cholesterol

Dijon mustard gives a pleasant tang without adding fat or calories.

2 tablespoons honey
1 tablespoon Dijon-style mustard
1 tablespoon lemon juice
½ teaspoon poppy seed
¼ teaspoon pepper

● In a small bowl combine honey, mustard, lemon juice, poppy seed, and pepper. Stir together well.

2 whole medium chicken breasts (about 1½ pounds total), skinned and halved lengthwise

● Rinse chicken; pat dry. Place chicken, bone side up, on the unheated rack of a broiler pan. Broil 4 to 5 inches from heat for 15 minutes. Turn. Continue broiling for 10 minutes. Brush with honey-mustard mixture. Broil about 5 minutes more or till tender and no longer pink. Makes 4 servings.

Nutrition information per serving: 168 calories, 1 g saturated fat, 1 g monounsaturated fat, 1 g polyunsaturated fat, 24 g protein, 9 g carbohydrate, 174 mg sodium, 210 mg potassium.

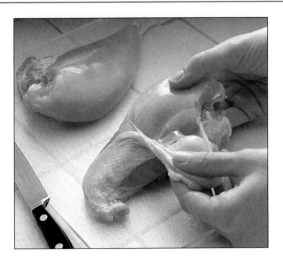

Pulling the skin off chicken is one of the easiest ways to get rid of fat. With the breasts and thighs, start at one end and pull the skin away from the meat. If necessary, slip a finger under the skin to loosen. With the legs and wings, run a knife under the skin and cut a slit in it, then pull the skin off.

After you've removed the skin, you'll see several pockets of cream-colored fat. Use a sharp knife to cut them off.

Lime-Glazed Turkey

3 g fat
59 mg cholesterol

¼ teaspoon finely shredded lime peel
  or lemon peel
2 tablespoons lime juice *or* lemon juice
1 tablespoon corn syrup
¼ teaspoon dried tarragon, crushed
¼ teaspoon paprika
⅛ teaspoon salt
⅛ teaspoon garlic powder
  Several dashes bottled hot pepper
  sauce

● For glaze, in a small bowl combine lime or lemon peel, lime or lemon juice, corn syrup, tarragon, paprika, salt, garlic powder, and hot pepper sauce. Mix well.

4 turkey breast tenderloin steaks,
  cut ½ inch thick

● Rinse turkey and pat dry. Cook on an uncovered grill directly over *medium* coals for 6 minutes. Turn and brush with glaze. Continue cooking for 6 to 9 minutes more or till tender and no longer pink, brushing frequently with glaze during the last few minutes.
  Or, to broil, place on the unheated rack of a broiler pan. Broil 4 to 5 inches from the heat for 5 minutes. Brush turkey with glaze. Turn and brush again with glaze. Continue broiling for 6 to 8 minutes more or till tender and no longer pink, brushing frequently with glaze during the last few minutes. Makes 4 servings.

Nutrition information per serving: 150 calories, 1 g saturated fat, 0 g monounsaturated fat, 1 g polyunsaturated fat, 26 g protein, 4 g carbohydrate, 124 mg sodium, 271 mg potassium.

Cherry Chicken

3 g fat
54 mg cholesterol

Dunk each bite of broiled chicken in a luscious cherry sauce.

2 whole medium chicken breasts
  (about 1½ pounds total), skinned,
  boned, and halved lengthwise, *or*
  4 turkey breast tenderloin steaks,
  cut ½ inch thick
1 tablespoon lemon juice

● Rinse chicken or turkey; pat dry. Place on the unheated rack of a broiler pan. Broil 4 to 5 inches from the heat for 6 minutes. Brush with some of the lemon juice. Turn poultry over. Brush with remaining lemon juice. Broil 6 to 9 minutes or till tender and no longer pink.

⅓ cup cherry *or* seedless red raspberry
  preserves
1 tablespoon lemon juice
  Dash ground allspice

● For sauce, in a small saucepan cook and stir the preserves, lemon juice, and allspice over low heat till melted. Remove from heat. Pass sauce with chicken or turkey. Makes 4 servings.

Nutrition information per serving: 183 calories, 1 g saturated fat, 1 g monounsaturated fat, 1 g polyunsaturated fat, 20 g protein, 19 g carbohydrate, 52 mg sodium, 191 mg potassium.

Turkey Kabobs

1 g fat
0 mg cholesterol

Red pepper and gingerroot give a pleasant zing to the turkey and vegetables.

⅓ **cup red wine vinegar**
3 **tablespoons corn syrup**
2 **tablespoons soy sauce**
1½ **teaspoons grated gingerroot**
¼ **teaspoon garlic powder**
¼ **teaspoon crushed red pepper**

● For marinade, in a medium bowl combine the vinegar, corn syrup, soy sauce, gingerroot, garlic powder, and red pepper.

12 **ounces turkey breast tenderloin steaks**

● Rinse turkey; pat dry. Cut lengthwise into ½-inch-wide strips. Add to marinade; stir to coat. Let stand at room temperature for 30 minutes or chill for 1 hour, stirring occasionally.

1 **small zucchini**
1 **small yellow crookneck squash**
1 **medium sweet red pepper**

● Cut zucchini and yellow squash into ¾-inch slices. Cut any large pieces in half. Cut red pepper into 1-inch squares.

Remove turkey from marinade, reserving marinade. On four 10- or 12-inch skewers, thread turkey strips, accordion-style, around zucchini, yellow squash, and pepper pieces.

Place on the unheated rack of a broiler pan. Broil 3 to 4 inches from the heat for 5 minutes. Brush turkey and vegetables with marinade; turn kabobs. Broil 3 to 5 minutes more or till turkey is no longer pink and vegetables are tender, brushing often with marinade.

Or, to grill, cook on an uncovered grill over *medium-hot* coals for 10 to 12 minutes or till turkey is no longer pink and vegetables are tender, turning and brushing often with marinade. Makes 4 servings.

Nutrition information per serving: 151 calories, 0 g saturated fat, 0 g monounsaturated fat, 0 g polyunsaturated fat, 20 g protein, 17 g carbohydrate, 556 mg sodium, 396 mg potassium.

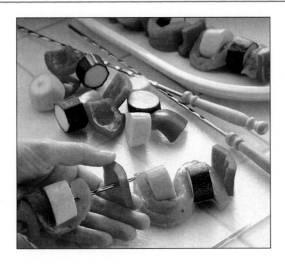

To thread kabobs accordion-style, start by placing one end of a turkey strip on a skewer. Add a vegetable piece, then loop the turkey around the vegetable and over the point of the skewer. Repeat with the remaining turkey and vegetables, being careful to leave a little space between each piece.

Turkey Stir-Fry

10 g fat
22 mg cholesterol

Creamy, herb-flavored sauce coats turkey strips and pasta.

½ **of an 8-ounce package Neufchâtel cheese, cubed**
¼ **cup skim milk**
¼ **cup dry white wine**
2 **teaspoons cornstarch**
¼ **teaspoon dried thyme, crushed**
¼ **teaspoon dried chervil, crushed**

● In a small mixing bowl combine cubed Neufchâtel cheese, milk, wine, cornstarch, thyme, chervil, ¼ teaspoon *salt,* and ¼ teaspoon *pepper.* Set aside.

1 **pound turkey breast tenderloin steaks *or* boned skinless chicken breast halves**
Nonstick spray coating
½ **cup bias-sliced celery**
½ **cup chopped sweet red pepper**
½ **cup chopped onion**

● Rinse turkey; pat dry. Cut into thin bite-size strips. Spray a *cold* wok or large skillet with nonstick coating. Preheat wok or skillet over medium-high heat. Then add celery, chopped pepper, and onion. Stir-fry for 1 minute.

1½ **cups sliced fresh mushrooms**
2 **teaspoons cooking oil**

● Add mushrooms to wok or skillet; stir-fry for 1 minute. Remove vegetables. Add *1 teaspoon* of the oil. Add *half* of the turkey to the wok or skillet. Stir-fry for 2 to 3 minutes or till turkey is no longer pink; remove turkey.

Add remaining oil. Stir-fry remaining turkey for 2 to 3 minutes or till no longer pink. Return all turkey and vegetables to wok or skillet.

8 **ounces fettuccine *or* linguine, cooked and drained**

● Add cheese mixture to wok or skillet; cook and stir till cheese melts and mixture is heated through. Arrange pasta on a platter. Top with turkey mixture. Serve immediately. Serves 4.

Nutrition information per serving: 333 calories, 5 g saturated fat, 3 g monounsaturated fat, 2 g polyunsaturated fat, 33 g protein, 24 g carbohydrate, 309 mg sodium, 552 mg potassium.

Olive Oil

Have you wondered why olive oil is sometimes recommended by health professionals? It's because olive oil contains a higher percent of monounsaturated fat than other vegetable oils. Some studies indicate that monounsaturated fats help some people lower their cholesterol levels.

Unless you've been advised by a dietitian to use only olive oil, you don't have to rely entirely on it. You might like to use both olive oil and another vegetable oil in your kitchen. The most important thing is to choose an oil that's low in saturated fat, such as corn, soybean, peanut, safflower, olive, or canola oil. And remember, whichever oil you choose, use it in moderation. They are all fats and have 125 calories per tablespoon.

Slim Saltimbocca

6 g fat
66 mg cholesterol

Baking instead of frying cuts the fat in this classic dish. And you'll still find the crisp coating and ham and cheese filling that makes saltimbocca popular.

2 whole medium chicken breasts (about 1½ pounds total), skinned, boned, and halved lengthwise

● Rinse chicken; pat dry. Place each half between two pieces of clear plastic wrap. Working from the center to the edges, pound lightly with the flat side of a meat mallet till ¼ inch thick. Remove wrap.

1 slice part-skim mozzarella cheese (1 ounce)
2 ounces very thinly sliced, fully cooked ham
1 small tomato, seeded and chopped

● Cut cheese into 4 pieces. Place *one-fourth* of the ham and *one* piece of the cheese on *each* chicken piece. Top *each* with *one-fourth* of the tomato. Roll up jelly-roll style, tucking in sides to seal well. Secure with wooden toothpicks.

3 tablespoons fine dry bread crumbs
1 tablespoon grated Parmesan cheese
1 tablespoon snipped parsley *or*
1 teaspoon parsley flakes
½ teaspoon dried oregano, crushed
⅛ teaspoon garlic powder
⅛ teaspoon pepper

● In a pie plate or on a sheet of waxed paper combine bread crumbs, Parmesan cheese, parsley, oregano, garlic powder, and pepper. Mix together.

1 tablespoon skim milk

● Brush chicken rolls with milk. Then roll in crumb mixture to coat well. Place in a 10x6x2-inch baking dish. Bake, uncovered, in a 350° oven about 25 minutes or till chicken is tender and no longer pink. Makes 4 servings.

Nutrition information per serving: 182 calories, 2 g saturated fat, 2 g monounsaturated fat, 1 g polyunsaturated fat, 26 g protein, 5 g carbohydrate, 360 mg sodium, 303 mg potassium.

Start rolling the chicken from one of the short sides. As you roll, tuck the sides in a little to seal in the cheese.

Fish Creole

2 g fat
42 mg cholesterol

You'll find plenty of peppy flavor in the sauce.

1 pound fresh *or* frozen red snapper, orange roughy, *or* other fish fillets **1 medium onion, chopped (½ cup)** **½ cup chopped green pepper** **½ cup chopped celery** **¼ cup water**	● Thaw fish, if frozen. Cut into 4 serving-size portions. Measure thickness of fish. In a large skillet combine chopped onion, green pepper, celery, and water. Bring to boiling; reduce heat. Simmer, covered, about 5 minutes or till vegetables are tender.
1 16-ounce can tomatoes, cut up **1 bay leaf** **2 tablespoons snipped parsley** **½ teaspoon garlic powder** **¼ teaspoon salt** **⅛ teaspoon ground red pepper**	● Stir in *undrained* tomatoes, bay leaf, parsley, garlic powder, salt, and red pepper. Bring to boiling; reduce heat. Simmer, covered, for 5 minutes. Add fish. Cook (allow 4 to 6 minutes per ½-inch thickness of fish) till fish just flakes when tested with a fork. With a slotted spatula, transfer fish to a platter. Cover to keep warm.
2 tablespoons cold water **1 tablespoon cornstarch** **2 cups hot cooked rice (optional)**	● Stir together water and cornstarch. Stir into tomato mixture. Cook and stir till thickened and bubbly, then cook and stir for 2 minutes more. Discard bay leaf. Serve over fish. Serve with rice, if desired. Makes 4 servings.

Nutrition information per serving: 157 calories, 0 g saturated fat, 0 g monounsaturated fat, 7 g polyunsaturated fat, 25 g protein. 10 g carbohydrate, 405 mg sodium, 836 mg potassium.

Dilled Fish Chowder

1 g fat
49 mg cholesterol

12 ounces fresh *or* frozen cod, haddock, *or* other fish fillets **1 large potato, peeled and cubed** **1 cup frozen cut green beans** **1 medium carrot, shredded** **1 medium onion, chopped** **1 tablespoon instant chicken bouillon granules** **1 teaspoon dried dillweed**	● Thaw fish, if frozen. Pat dry. Cut fish into 1-inch pieces. In a large saucepan combine potato, frozen beans, carrot, onion, bouillon granules, dillweed, 1½ cups *water,* and ¼ teaspoon *pepper.* Bring to boiling; reduce heat. Simmer, covered, for 5 to 10 minutes or till potato is tender.
2½ cups skim milk **3 tablespoons cornstarch**	● Combine ½ *cup* of the milk and cornstarch. Add to vegetables. Add remaining milk and fish. Cook and stir gently till boiling; reduce heat. Cook and stir for 2 to 3 minutes more or till thickened and fish just flakes. Serves 4.

Nutrition information per serving: 222 calories, 0 g saturated fat, 0 g monounsaturated fat, 0 g polyunsaturated fat, 26 g protein, 26 g carbohydrate, 833 mg sodium, 710 mg potassium.

Fish Creole

Orange-Honey Fish

1 g fat
47 mg cholesterol

1 pound fresh *or* frozen orange roughy, grouper, cod, *or* other fish fillets

● Thaw fish, if frozen. Pat dry. Cut into 4 serving-size portions. Measure thickness of fish.

2 tablespoons finely chopped green onion
1 teaspoon finely shredded orange peel
2 tablespoons orange juice
2 tablespoons honey
½ teaspoon paprika

● For glaze, in a small bowl stir together onion, orange peel, orange juice, honey, paprika, ¼ teaspoon *salt,* and ⅛ teaspoon *pepper.*

Orange slices (optional)

● Place fish on the unheated rack of a broiler pan. Brush some of the glaze over fish. Broil 4 inches from the heat (allow 4 to 6 minutes per ½-inch thickness) till fish just flakes with a fork, brushing occasionally with glaze. Garnish with orange slices, if desired. Makes 4 servings.

Nutrition information per serving: 127 calories, 0 g saturated fat, 0 g monounsaturated fat, 0 g polyunsaturated fat, 20 g protein, 10 g carbohydrate, 200 mg sodium, 245 mg potassium.

Lemon-Fennel Fish

2 g fat
58 mg cholesterol

Sprinkling lemon juice on the fish instead of brushing it with butter moistens and flavors it.

Nonstick spray coating
1 pound skinless flounder, orange roughy, *or* sole fillets, cut ¼ inch to ¾ inch thick
1 to 2 tablespoons lemon juice

● Spray a 10x6x2- or 12x7½x2-inch baking dish with nonstick coating. Measure thickness of fish. Arrange thick fillets in a single layer in the baking dish, tucking under any of the thin edges. *Or,* stack thin fillets evenly in the dish. Sprinkle with lemon juice.

¼ cup fine dry bread crumbs
½ teaspoon fennel seed, crushed
½ teaspoon finely shredded lemon peel
¼ teaspoon paprika
Dash pepper

● Stir together bread crumbs, fennel seed, lemon peel, paprika, and pepper; sprinkle over fish. Bake in a 450° oven (allow 6 to 8 minutes per ½-inch thickness of fish) till fish just flakes with a fork. Makes 4 servings.

Nutrition information per serving: 128 calories, 0 g saturated fat, 0 g monounsaturated fat, 0 g polyunsaturated fat, 21 g protein, 5 g carbohydrate, 135 mg sodium, 315 mg potassium.

 Microwave Directions: In a microwave-safe dish arrange fish as directed above. Sprinkle with lemon juice. Cover with vented microwave-safe plastic wrap. Micro-cook fish on 100% power (high) for 3 minutes. Drain well.

Meanwhile, prepare crumb mixture as above. Sprinkle crumb mixture over fish. Cook, uncovered, on high for 1 to 3 minutes or till fish just flakes when tested with a fork, rotating dish a half-turn once.

Poached Salmon Steaks

6 g fat
89 mg cholesterol

A delicate wine-mustard sauce is the perfect accent for salmon steaks. (Pictured on the cover.)

**4 fresh *or* frozen salmon *or* halibut
   steaks, cut 1 inch thick (about
   1½ pounds total)**
½ cup water
½ cup dry white wine
1 green onion, sliced
1 bay leaf

● Thaw fish, if frozen. In a large skillet combine water, wine, green onion, and bay leaf. Bring to boiling. Add fish steaks. Return just to boiling; reduce heat. Simmer, covered, for 8 to 12 minutes or till fish just flakes when tested with a fork. Discard bay leaf. Remove fish from skillet; cover to keep warm.

⅓ cup skim milk
1 tablespoon Dijon-style mustard
2 teaspoons cornstarch
**1 teaspoon white wine Worcestershire
   sauce**
Lemon slices (optional)
Fresh dillweed (optional)

● For sauce, gently boil liquid in skillet till reduced to ½ cup. Combine milk, mustard, cornstarch, and white wine Worcestershire sauce. Add to liquid in skillet. Cook and stir over medium heat till thickened and bubbly. Cook and stir for 2 minutes more.

Spoon sauce over fish. Garnish with lemon slices and sprigs of fresh dillweed, if desired. Makes 4 servings.

Nutrition information per serving: 237 calories, 1 g saturated fat, 2 g monounsaturated fat, 2 g polyunsaturated fat, 35 g protein, 2 g carbohydrate, 256 mg sodium, 605 mg potassium.

To see if fish is done, insert a fork into the thickest part at a 45-degree angle. Twist the fork gently and pull up some of the flesh. If it just flakes and looks opaque, the fish is just right. If it resists flaking and looks translucent, it isn't done. Continue cooking and testing frequently until the fish tests done.

Scallop Stir-Fry

6 g fat
37 mg cholesterol

If you don't have a wok, a large skillet with high sides works well.

1 **pound fresh *or* frozen scallops**
¾ **pound fresh asparagus *or* one**
    10-ounce package frozen cut
    asparagus
¼ **cup dry white wine**
2 **tablespoons soy sauce *or* sodium-**
    reduced soy sauce
1 **tablespoon cornstarch**
	● Thaw scallops, if frozen. Cut any large scallops into bite-size pieces. Snap off and discard woody bases from fresh asparagus. Bias-slice into 1-inch lengths. Set aside.
	    For sauce, stir together white wine, soy sauce, cornstarch, and ¼ cup *cold water*. Set aside.

Nonstick spray coating 1 **teaspoon grated gingerroot** 2 **teaspoons cooking oil** 1 **cup sliced fresh mushrooms**	● Spray a *cold* wok or large skillet with nonstick coating. Preheat wok over medium-high heat. Stir-fry gingerroot in wok for 15 seconds. Add asparagus. Stir-fry for 4 minutes. (If using frozen asparagus, stir-fry 2 minutes.) Add oil *1 teaspoon* at a time as necessary. Add mushrooms. Stir-fry 2 minutes or till asparagus is crisp-tender. Remove vegetables from wok.
2 **cups hot cooked rice**	● Add *half* of the scallops to the wok. Stir-fry about 3 minutes or till opaque. Remove scallops. Repeat with remaining scallops; remove from wok. Add sauce to wok. Cook and stir till thickened and bubbly. Cook and stir 1 minute more. Return vegetables and scallops to wok. Cook and stir 1 minute. Serve over rice. Makes 4 servings.

Nutrition information per serving: 295 calories, 1 g saturated fat, 1 g monounsaturated fat, 3 g polyunsaturated fat, 24 g protein, 33 g carbohydrate, 688 mg sodium, 700 mg potassium.

Tuna Tabouleh

3 g fat
35 mg cholesterol

¾ **cup bulgur**	● Rinse bulgur in a colander with cold water. Drain well.

1 **6½-ounce can tuna (water pack),**
    drained and flaked
1 **small tomato, seeded and chopped**
½ **cup chopped cucumber**
¼ **cup snipped parsley**
2 **green onions, sliced**
⅛ **teaspoon pepper**
⅔ **cup reduced-calorie Italian salad**
    dressing
3 **lettuce leaves**
	● In a medium bowl combine bulgur, tuna, chopped tomato, cucumber, parsley, green onion, and pepper. Pour dressing over bulgur mixture; toss gently to coat. Cover and chill at least 4 hours before serving. Serve on 3 lettuce-lined plates. Makes 3 servings.

Nutrition information per serving: 268 calories, 1 g saturated fat, 1 g monounsaturated fat, 1 g polyunsaturated fat, 22 g protein, 38 g carbohydrate, 633 mg sodium, 459 mg potassium.

Tuna Burgers

5 g fat
54 mg cholesterol

Enjoy this fat-slashed version of a family favorite.

2 egg whites
2 tablespoons skim milk
1 cup soft bread crumbs
2 tablespoons chopped dill pickle
1 teaspoon dried minced onion
¼ teaspoon paprika
2 6½-ounce cans tuna (water pack)

● In a medium bowl stir together egg whites and skim milk. Stir in bread crumbs, pickle, onion, paprika, and ⅛ teaspoon *pepper*.
   Drain tuna and break into chunks. Add tuna to crumb mixture; mix well. Shape into four ½-inch-thick patties.

Nonstick spray coating

● Spray a shallow baking pan with nonstick coating; add patties. Broil 4 inches from the heat 6 to 8 minutes or till brown, turning once.

4 whole wheat hamburger buns
4 teaspoons reduced-calorie
    mayonnaise *or* salad dressing
4 lettuce leaves
4 tomato slices

● Spread bottom of *each* bun with *1* teaspoon mayonnaise or salad dressing. Line each with a lettuce leaf. Top with tuna patty, tomato slice, and bun top. Makes 4 servings.

Nutrition information per serving: 319 calories, 1 g saturated fat, 1 g monounsaturated fat, 2 g polyunsaturated fat, 34 g protein, 31 g carbohydrate, 815 mg sodium, 520 mg potassium.

Tuna Cheese Burgers
2 1-ounce slices part-skim mozzarella
    cheese, halved

Prepare Tuna Burgers as above, *except* top broiled patties with a piece of cheese. Broil about 30 seconds or till cheese is just melted.

Nutrition information per serving: 355 calories, 8 g total fat (3 g saturated fat, 2 g monounsaturated fat, 2 g polyunsaturated fat), 62 mg cholesterol, 38 g protein, 32 g carbohydrate, 881 mg sodium, 532 mg potassium.

Bunless Tuna Burgers

Prepare Tuna Burgers as above, *except* omit buns. Serve patties on lettuce with tomato.

Nutrition information per serving: 201 calories, 3 g total fat (1 g saturated fat, 0 g monounsaturated fat, 1 g polyunsaturated fat), 54 mg cholesterol, 31 g protein, 11 g carbohydrate, 550 mg sodium, 578 mg potassium.

Omega-3 and Fish

Omega-3 fatty acids are substances that may lower blood cholesterol levels, and some fish contain more than others. Among the best sources of omega-3 fatty acids are lake and rainbow trout, mackerel, salmon, herring, tuna, and swordfish.

Dijon Seafood Salad

10 g fat
15 mg cholesterol

Get delicious seafood flavor without high cholesterol by using crab- or shrimp-flavored fish. Look for either product in the frozen food section or the deli.

1 8-ounce package frozen crab- *or* **shrimp-flavored, salad-style fish**

● Thaw crab- *or* shrimp-flavored fish. Cut any large pieces into bite-size pieces.

¼ cup low-fat plain yogurt
¼ cup reduced-calorie mayonnaise *or* **salad dressing**
2 tablespoons skim milk
1 tablespoon snipped chives
2 teaspoons Dijon-style mustard

● For dressing, in a small bowl stir together yogurt, mayonnaise or salad dressing, milk, chives, and Dijon-style mustard.

4 cups shredded lettuce
1 15-ounce can garbanzo beans, chilled and drained
¼ cup chopped green *or* **sweet red pepper**
1 medium cucumber, thinly sliced

● Line 3 plates with shredded lettuce. Combine garbanzo beans and chopped pepper; place a *third* of the bean mixture in the center of *each* plate. Arrange cucumber slices and fish around bean mixture. Drizzle dressing over salads. Makes 3 servings.

Nutrition information per serving: 372 calories, 2 g saturated fat, 1 g monounsaturated fat, 5 g polyunsaturated fat, 21 g protein, 49 g carbohydrate, 685 mg sodium, 677 mg potassium.

Arranging the salads individually, rather than passing a salad bowl, helps to divide the portions equally. Plus, they look extra special without much effort.

Pasta with Clam Sauce

5 g fat
33 mg cholesterol

Entertain without blowing your low-fat resolution. Just feature this pasta dish with a tossed salad, steamed asparagus, Italian bread, and white wine.

2 6½-ounce cans minced clams

● Drain clams, reserving ½ *cup* clam liquid. Set aside.

⅓ cup chopped onion
2 cloves garlic, minced
1 tablespoon olive oil *or* cooking oil
⅓ cup dry white wine
**½ teaspoon dried basil *or* oregano,
      crushed**
Dash ground red pepper

● In a medium skillet cook onion and garlic in hot olive or cooking oil about 4 minutes or till onion is tender. Carefully add reserved clam liquid, wine, basil or oregano, and red pepper. Bring to boiling and boil gently for 4 minutes. Reduce heat; add clams. Simmer for 2 minutes, stirring occasionally.

8 ounces linguine *or* spaghetti
3 tablespoons snipped parsley

● Meanwhile, cook pasta in boiling salted water according to package directions. Drain. Return pasta to hot pan. Add clam mixture and parsley. Toss gently till well coated. Serve immediately. Makes 4 servings.

Nutrition information per serving: 204 calories, 1 g saturated fat, 3 g monounsaturated fat, 1 g polyunsaturated fat, 16 g protein, 21 g carbohydrate, 150 mg sodium, 395 mg potassium.

Seaside Pasta Soup

2 g fat
38 mg cholesterol

Parmesan cheese is like an ace in the hole—use it to add flavor and stay within low-fat limits.

1½ cups water
**1 10-ounce package frozen Italian
      cut green beans**
⅓ cup tiny shell macaroni
2 green onions, sliced
2 teaspoons sugar
1 teaspoon dried thyme, crushed
¼ teaspoon garlic powder
¼ teaspoon pepper

● In a large saucepan combine water, beans, uncooked macaroni, green onion, sugar, thyme, garlic powder, and pepper.
Bring to boiling. Reduce heat. Cook, covered, for 6 to 8 minutes or till the macaroni is tender, stirring occasionally. *Do not drain.*

1 28-ounce can tomatoes, cut up
**1 9¼-ounce can tuna (water pack)
      or one 6½-ounce can skinless,
      boneless salmon, drained and
      broken into chunks**
4 teaspoons grated Parmesan cheese

● Stir in *undrained* tomatoes and tuna or salmon; heat through.
Ladle soup into 4 bowls. Sprinkle *each* serving with *1 teaspoon* of the Parmesan cheese. Makes 4 servings.

Nutrition information per serving: 203 calories, 1 g saturated fat, 0 g monounsaturated fat, 0 g polyunsaturated fat, 24 g protein, 24 g carbohydrate, 597 mg sodium, 754 mg potassium.

Hamburger Pizza

14 g fat
39 mg cholesterol

Have your pizza and low-fat fare, too. Just use beef instead of sausage or pepperoni, and reduce the cheese a little.

1¼ **cups all-purpose flour**
1 **package active dry yeast**
½ **teaspoon salt**
1 **cup warm water (120° to 130°)**
2 **tablespoons cooking oil**
1½ **to 2 cups whole wheat flour**

● In a large mixer bowl combine all-purpose flour, yeast, and salt. Add warm water and oil. Beat with an electric mixer on low to medium speed for 30 seconds, scraping sides of bowl constantly. Beat on high speed for 3 minutes. Using a spoon, stir in as much whole wheat flour as you can.

Turn out onto a lightly floured surface. Knead in enough of the remaining whole wheat flour to make a moderately stiff dough that is smooth and elastic (6 to 8 minutes total). Divide in half. Cover and let rest 10 minutes.

8 **ounces lean ground beef**
1 **cup sliced fresh mushrooms**
1 **cup chopped green pepper**
1 **small onion, thinly sliced and separated into rings**
1 **clove garlic, minced**
¼ **teaspoon crushed red pepper (optional)**

● Meanwhile, in a medium skillet cook ground beef, mushrooms, green pepper, onion, and garlic till meat is brown and vegetables are tender. Drain well in a colander. Stir in red pepper, if desired. Set aside.

Nonstick spray coating
2 **tablespoons cornmeal**
1 **15-ounce can pizza sauce**
1½ **cups shredded part-skim mozzarella cheese (6 ounces)**

● Spray two 12-inch pizza pans or baking sheets with nonstick coating. Sprinkle each pan with cornmeal. On a lightly floured surface, roll each half of dough into a 13-inch circle. Transfer to pans. Build up edges slightly. *Do not let rise.* Bake in a 425° oven about 12 minutes or till browned.

Spread pizza sauce over hot crust. Sprinkle meat mixture over sauce. Sprinkle with cheese. Bake 10 to 15 minutes more or till the top is bubbly. Makes 6 servings.

To freeze: After assembling pizzas, cool and wrap in clear plastic wrap, then cover with foil. Freeze. To serve, remove plastic wrap. Cover loosely with foil. Bake frozen pizzas in a 425° oven for 10 minutes. Uncover and bake 12 to 15 minutes more or till heated through.

Nutrition information per serving: 426 calories, 4 g saturated fat, 3 g monounsaturated fat, 3 g polyunsaturated fat, 25 g protein, 52 g carbohydrate, 629 mg sodium, 390 mg potassium.

Hamburger Pie

11 g fat
50 mg cholesterol

We adapted this popular recipe by substituting tomatoes for the tomato soup and omitting the cheese garnish.

1 pound lean ground beef

● In a large skillet cook ground beef till brown. Drain well in a strainer or colander. Wipe skillet with paper towels. Return beef to the skillet.

2 14½-ounce cans stewed tomatoes
½ of a 6-ounce can (⅓ cup) tomato paste
1 tablespoon dried minced onion
½ teaspoon dried basil, crushed
1 10-ounce package frozen peas and carrots

● Stir stewed tomatoes, tomato paste, minced onion, and basil into meat in the skillet. Stir in frozen peas and carrots.
　Bring to boiling; reduce heat. Simmer, covered, about 10 minutes or till peas and carrots are crisp-tender. Uncover and simmer for 3 to 5 minutes more or till desired consistency.

Packaged instant mashed potatoes (enough for 4 servings)
Snipped parsley

● Meanwhile, prepare instant mashed potatoes according to package directions, *except* use *skim milk* and omit margarine or butter. Drop potatoes into six mounds atop beef mixture. Sprinkle with parsley. Makes 6 servings.

Nutrition information per serving: 391 calories, 4 g saturated fat, 5 g monounsaturated fat, 1 g polyunsaturated fat, 21 g protein, 54 g carbohydrate, 703 mg sodium, 716 mg potassium.

To thoroughly drain fat from browned ground meats, set a strainer or colander over a bowl or disposable container. Spoon the meat into the strainer. Let the meat stand a few minutes, then give the strainer a few shakes. Patting the meat dry with paper towels and wiping the skillet with towels will eliminate even more fat.

Eye of Round with Salsa

7 g fat
69 mg cholesterol

The salsa also is great with slices of cold cooked beef, turkey, or chicken.

1 2-pound beef eye of round roast

● Trim fat from roast. Place roast on a rack in a shallow roasting pan. Insert a meat thermometer in the center of the roast. Roast, uncovered, in a 325° oven for 1¼ to 1¾ hours or till thermometer registers 140° for rare or for 1¾ to 2¼ hours or till thermometer register 160° for medium.

Remove roast from oven. Cover with foil and let stand for 15 minutes before carving.

Or, to cook roast on a grill, in a covered grill arrange *medium* coals around a drip pan. Test for *medium-low* heat above the pan. Place roast on grill rack over drip pan but not over coals. Insert a meat thermometer. Lower the grill hood. Grill for 1 to 1¼ hours or till meat thermometer registers 140° for rare or for 1½ to 2 hours or till thermometer registers 160° for medium.

Pineapple Salsa

● Serve Pineapple Salsa with sliced roast. Makes 8 servings.

Nutrition information per serving: 216 calories, 2 g saturated fat, 3 g monounsaturated fat, 0 g polyunsaturated fat, 25 g protein, 13 g carbohydrate, 145 mg sodium, 458 mg potassium.

Pineapple Salsa
2 8¼-ounce cans crushed pineapple, drained
2 medium tomatoes, peeled, seeded, and chopped
2 tablespoons lime *or* lemon juice
2 teaspoons sugar
2 teaspoons soy sauce
1 teaspoon garlic powder
1 teaspoon dry mustard
   Several dashes bottled hot pepper sauce

In a bowl place the pineapple, tomatoes, lime or lemon juice, sugar, soy sauce, garlic powder, dry mustard, and hot pepper sauce. Stir together to combine. Makes 8 servings.

Nutrition information per serving: 171 calories, 0 g total fat (0 g saturated fat, 0 g monounsaturated fat, 0 g polyunsaturated fat), 0 mg cholesterol, 3 g protein, 43 g carbohydrate, 358 mg sodium, 543 mg potassium.

Beef and Beer Soup

8 g fat
61 mg cholesterol

Each spicy spoonful contains beef, vegetables, and lots of Tex-Mex flavor.

Nonstick spray coating	● Spray a *cold* large saucepan or Dutch oven with nonstick coating. Preheat the saucepan. Cook and stir beef, onion, and chili powder over medium-high heat till meat is brown.
¾ **pound boneless beef round steak, cut into ¾-inch cubes**	
1 **medium onion, chopped (½ cup)**	
1 **tablespoon chili powder**	
1 **16-ounce can tomatoes, cut up**	● Stir in *undrained* tomatoes, beer, chili peppers, bouillon granules, sugar, and ½ cup *water*. Bring to boiling; reduce heat. Simmer, covered, for 1 hour.
1 **12-ounce can beer**	
1 **4-ounce can diced green chili peppers**	
2 **teaspoons instant beef bouillon granules**	
1 **teaspoon sugar**	
1 **15½-ounce can red kidney beans, drained**	● Stir in kidney beans and corn. Cook, covered, for 10 to 15 minutes more or till the beef is tender. Combine water and cornstarch. Add to beef mixture. Cook and stir till thickened and bubbly. Cook and stir for 2 minutes more. Makes 4 servings.
1 **12-ounce can whole kernel corn, drained**	
2 **tablespoons cold water**	
1 **tablespoon cornstarch**	

Nutrition information per serving: 424 calories, 3 g saturated fat, 3 g monounsaturated fat, 1 g polyunsaturated fat, 33 g protein, 52 g carbohydrate, 893 mg sodium, 1,114 mg potassium.

Zippy Beef Sandwiches

9 g fat
46 mg cholesterol

Alfalfa sprouts add a touch of freshness to this beef and bean sandwich.

½ **pound lean ground beef**	● In large skillet cook beef and onion till brown. Drain (see photo, page 72). Wipe skillet with paper towels. Return mixture to skillet.
1 **medium onion, chopped (½ cup)**	
1 **8-ounce can red kidney beans**	● Stir *undrained* kidney beans, tomato sauce, brown sugar, mustard, Worcestershire sauce, hot pepper sauce, and dash *pepper* into meat mixture. Bring to boiling; reduce heat. Simmer, covered, for 10 minutes. Then, simmer, uncovered, 3 minutes or till desired consistency.
1 **8-ounce can tomato sauce**	
1 **tablespoon brown sugar**	
1 **tablespoon prepared mustard**	
1 **teaspoon Worcestershire sauce**	
Few dashes bottled hot pepper sauce	
4 **French rolls *or* Kaiser rolls, split and toasted**	● Spoon meat mixture into rolls. Top with alfalfa sprouts or shredded lettuce, if desired. Makes 4 servings.
1 **cup alfalfa sprouts *or* shredded lettuce (optional)**	

Nutrition information per serving: 306 calories, 3 g saturated fat, 4 g monounsaturated fat, 1 g polyunsaturated fat, 21 g protein, 36 g carbohydrate, 835 mg sodium, 566 mg potassium.

Spiced Beef Roast

5 g fat
52 mg cholesterol

Mushrooms in a creamy Dijon mustard sauce top each serving.

¼ teaspoon fennel seed
¼ teaspoon mustard seed
¼ teaspoon whole black peppers
1 2- to 2½-pound boneless beef
    round rump roast

● Using a mortar and pestle, crush the fennel seed, mustard seed, and peppers. Set aside.
   Trim fat from roast. Place roast on rack in shallow roasting pan. Rub seed mixture over top and sides of roast. Insert a meat thermometer in the center of the roast. Roast, uncovered, in a 325° oven for 1¼ to 1¾ hours or till a meat thermometer registers 150° to 170°. Remove roast from oven. Cover with foil and let stand for 15 minutes before carving.

1 cup sliced fresh mushrooms
1 cup skim milk
1 tablespoon cornstarch
½ teaspoon instant beef bouillon
    granules
1 tablespoon Dijon-style mustard
1 teaspoon snipped chives

● Meanwhile, for sauce, in a small saucepan cook mushrooms in a small amount of boiling water about 3 minutes or till tender. Drain. Stir together milk, cornstarch, and bouillon granules. Stir milk mixture into the mushrooms. Cook and stir till thickened and bubbly. Cook and stir for 2 minutes more. Stir in mustard and chives. Serve with roast. Makes 8 servings.

Nutrition information per serving: 155 calories, 2 g saturated fat, 2 g monounsaturated fat, 0 g polyunsaturated fat, 23 g protein, 3 g carbohydrate, 178 mg sodium, 381 mg potassium.

Swiss Steak

9 g fat
81 mg cholesterol

1 pound boneless beef round steak,
    cut ¾ inch thick
Nonstick spray coating

● Trim fat from steak. Cut into 4 serving-size pieces. Spray a *cold* 12-inch skillet with nonstick coating. Preheat skillet. Brown steak on both sides. Wipe skillet with paper towels.

1 28-ounce can tomatoes, cut up
1 small onion, sliced and separated
    into rings
½ cup sliced celery
1 bay leaf
1½ teaspoons dried marjoram, crushed
¼ teaspoon salt
⅛ teaspoon pepper
1 tablespoon cornstarch
1 tablespoon cold water
2 cups hot cooked rice *or* fettuccine

● Return steak to skillet. Add *undrained* tomatoes, onion, celery, bay leaf, marjoram, salt, and pepper. Bring to boiling; reduce heat. Simmer, covered, about 1¼ hours or till meat is tender. Remove meat from skillet; keep warm. Discard bay leaf.
   For sauce, mix cornstarch and water; stir into tomato mixture. Cook and stir till thickened and bubbly. Cook and stir 2 minutes more. Serve meat and sauce over rice or fettuccine. Serves 4.

Nutrition information per serving: 357 calories, 3 g saturated fat, 4 g monounsaturated fat, 1 g polyunsaturated fat, 31 g protein, 37 g carbohydrate, 513 mg sodium, 797 mg potassium.

Pork Chops and Apples

9 g fat
71 mg cholesterol

Sage-seasoned pork chops topped with apples in a cider sauce and served with brown rice add up to a sensational meal.

4 pork loin chops, cut ½ inch thick
½ teaspoon dried sage, crushed
Nonstick spray coating
1 small onion, sliced and separated into rings

● Trim fat from chops. Rub sage onto both sides of chops.
  Spray a *cold* 12-inch skillet with nonstick coating. Preheat skillet. Cook chops for 5 minutes. Turn chops and add onion. Cook for 5 to 7 minutes more or till no pink remains. Remove chops and onion; keep chops warm. Wipe out skillet with paper towels.

2 apples, cored and cut into thin wedges
1 cup apple cider *or* apple juice
1 teaspoon brown sugar

● For sauce, in same skillet mix onion, apple wedges, cider or juice, and brown sugar. Bring to boiling; reduce heat. Simmer, covered, for 3 to 5 minutes or till apples are crisp-tender.

1 tablespoon cold water
2 teaspoons cornstarch
2 cups hot cooked brown rice

● Combine water and cornstarch. Add to skillet mixture. Cook and stir till thickened and bubbly. Cook and stir for 2 minutes more. Serve pork chops and apple mixture with brown rice. Makes 4 servings.

Nutrition information per serving: 367 calories, 3 g saturated fat, 4 g monounsaturated fat, 1 g polyunsaturated fat, 26 g protein, 46 g carbohydrate, 59 mg sodium, 550 mg potassium.

Ham Kabobs

6 g fat
35 mg cholesterol

Just five ingredients are needed for this one-dish meal on a stick.

4 tiny new potatoes (about ½ pound)

● Scrub and quarter potatoes. Cook, covered, in lightly salted, boiling water for 10 to 15 minutes or till tender. Drain and cool.

¾ pound lean fully cooked ham, cut into 1-inch cubes
1 medium green pepper, cut into 1-inch pieces
⅓ cup reduced-calorie French *or* Russian salad dressing
8 cherry tomatoes

● On eight 8- or 9-inch skewers, alternately thread potatoes, ham, and green pepper. Place kabobs on the unheated rack of a broiler pan. Brush with some of the salad dressing.
  Broil 4 inches from the heat about 10 minutes or till heated through, turning once and brushing with salad dressing twice. Place one cherry tomato on the end of each kabob. Makes 4 servings.

Nutrition information per serving: 207 calories, 1 g saturated fat, 2 g monounsaturated fat, 2 g polyunsaturated fat, 18 g protein, 20 g carbohydrate, 1,250 mg sodium, 574 mg potassium.

**Pork Chops
and Apples**

Pork Stew

10 g fat
58 mg cholesterol

It's a just-right blend of pork, sweet potatoes, and seasonings.

¾ **pound lean boneless pork**
Nonstick spray coating

● Trim fat from pork. Cut into ½-inch cubes. Spray a *cold* Dutch oven with nonstick coating. Preheat the Dutch oven. Add pork. Cook and stir till pork is brown. Drain. Wipe Dutch oven with paper towels.

1 **large onion, chopped (1 cup)**
1 **bay leaf**
1 **tablespoon instant beef bouillon**
  granules
½ **teaspoon dried thyme, crushed**
½ **teaspoon paprika**
⅛ **teaspoon garlic powder**
1¼ **pounds sweet potatoes (4 small),**
  peeled and cubed

● Carefully add 2½ cups *water* to the Dutch oven. Stir in onion, bay leaf, bouillon granules, thyme, paprika, garlic powder, and ¼ teaspoon *pepper.* Bring to boiling; reduce heat. Simmer, covered, for 30 minutes.
  Stir in sweet potatoes. Return to boiling; reduce heat. Simmer, covered, about 10 minutes or till potatoes are nearly tender.

1 **tablespoon cornstarch**
1 **tablespoon cold water**
1 **10-ounce package frozen peas**

● Stir together cornstarch and water. Stir into pork mixture. Add peas. Cook and stir till thickened and bubbly. Cook and stir for 2 minutes more. Discard bay leaf. Serves 4.

Nutrition information per serving: 388 calories, 3 g saturated fat, 4 g monounsaturated fat, 1 g polyunsaturated fat, 23 g protein, 50 g carbohydrate, 824 mg sodium, 686 mg potassium.

Encore Pork Salad

11 g fat
51 mg cholesterol

This combination of kidney or garbanzo beans and leftover meat makes a hearty salad.

1 **16-ounce can red kidney beans**
  or **garbanzo beans, chilled**
8 **ounces cubed lean cooked pork,**
  chicken, turkey, *or* beef (1½ cups)
½ **cup sliced celery**
¼ **cup chopped onion**
¼ **cup chopped green *or* sweet yellow**
  pepper
⅓ **cup reduced-calorie Russian**
  or **French salad dressing**
4 **cups shredded lettuce**
2 **tomatoes, cut into wedges**
  Green pepper rings (optional)

● Drain beans. In a large bowl combine beans, cubed meat, celery, onion, and green or yellow pepper. Add dressing and toss to coat.
  Arrange lettuce on 4 salad plates. Top with pork mixture and tomatoes. Garnish with green pepper rings, if desired. Makes 4 servings.

Nutrition information per serving: 330 calories, 3 g saturated fat, 4 g monounsaturated fat, 3 g polyunsaturated fat, 26 g protein, 32 g carbohydrate, 460 mg sodium, 927 mg potassium.

Lentil-Ham Soup

3 g fat
26 mg cholesterol

1 cup dry lentils **4 cups water**	● Rinse lentils. In a 4-quart Dutch oven combine lentils and water.
2 cups cubed lean fully cooked ham (10 ounces) **3 medium carrots, coarsely chopped** **1 medium onion, chopped (½ cup)** **1 bay leaf** **¼ teaspoon pepper** **¼ teaspoon dried marjoram, crushed** **⅛ teaspoon garlic powder**	● Stir cubed ham, carrots, onion, bay leaf, pepper, marjoram, and garlic powder into the Dutch oven. Bring to boiling; reduce heat. Simmer, covered, about 30 minutes or till lentils are tender.
1 16-ounce can tomatoes, cut up **3 tablespoons snipped parsley**	● Stir in *undrained* tomatoes and parsley. Heat through. Discard bay leaf. Serves 6.

Nutrition information per serving: 217 calories, 1 g saturated fat, 1 g monounsaturated fat, 1 g polyunsaturated fat, 22 g protein, 26 g carbohydrate, 759 mg sodium, 753 mg potassium.

Black Beans with Rice

2 g fat
0 mg cholesterol

Adopt this southern favorite as one of your standbys for a low-fat, high-fiber meal.

1½ cups dry black beans **6 cups water**	● Rinse beans. In a 4-quart Dutch oven combine black beans and water. Bring to boiling. Reduce heat. Simmer for 2 minutes. Remove from the heat. Cover; let stand for 1 hour. (*Or,* soak beans in a covered bowl overnight.) Drain and rinse beans.
2 cups chicken broth **2 large onions, chopped (2 cups)** **1 large green pepper, chopped (1 cup)** **2 stalks celery, chopped (1 cup)** **2 cloves garlic, minced** **2 bay leaves** **2 teaspoons dried oregano, crushed** **1 teaspoon salt** **¼ to ½ teaspoon crushed red pepper** **1 16-ounce can tomatoes, cut up**	● In the same Dutch oven combine the beans, broth, chopped onion, green pepper, celery, garlic, bay leaves, oregano, salt, and red pepper. Bring to boiling; reduce heat. Simmer, covered, for 2 to 2½ hours or till the black beans are tender, stirring in *undrained* tomatoes the last 15 minutes of cooking. Discard bay leaves. Mash beans slightly.
2 tablespoons lemon juice **2½ cups hot cooked rice** **¼ cup chopped onion**	● To serve, stir in lemon juice. Ladle beans into 5 soup dishes. Spoon rice atop beans. Sprinkle with chopped onion. Makes 5 servings.

Nutrition information per serving: 364 calories, 0 g saturated fat, 0 g monounsaturated fat, 1 g polyunsaturated fat, 18 g protein, 70 g carbohydrate, 909 mg sodium, 1,039 mg potassium.

Vegetable Lasagna

8 g fat
57 mg cholesterol

---

6 lasagna noodles

● Cook lasagna noodles according to package directions. Drain. Rinse with cold water. Drain again; set aside.

---

2 slightly beaten egg whites
1½ cups low-fat cottage cheese, drained
1 10-ounce package frozen chopped broccoli *or* one 9-ounce package frozen French-style green beans

● Stir together egg whites, cottage cheese, and ⅛ teaspoon *pepper.* Set aside.
  Cook broccoli or green beans according to package directions. Drain; set aside.

---

4 green onions, sliced
¼ cup water
1 cup skim milk
4 teaspoons cornstarch
½ teaspoon dried dillweed
Dash pepper
1 cup shredded part-skim mozzarella cheese (4 ounces)

● For sauce, in a medium saucepan cook green onions in water, covered, about 3 minutes or till tender. Combine skim milk, cornstarch, dillweed, and pepper. Add all at once to green onion mixture. Cook and stir till bubbly. Cook and stir for 1 minute more. Gradually add mozzarella cheese, stirring till melted. Stir in broccoli or green beans.

Nonstick spray coating
½ cup grated Parmesan cheese

● Spray a 10x6x2-inch baking dish with nonstick coating. Place *two* of the noodles in the dish (if necessary, cut noodles to fit dish). Spread *one-third* of the cottage cheese mixture over noodles. Top with *one-third* of the sauce. Then, sprinkle with *one-third* of the Parmesan cheese. Repeat layers 2 more times. Cover the dish with foil.
  Bake in a 350° oven for 30 minutes. Remove foil. Bake for 5 to 10 minutes more or till heated through. Let stand 10 minutes before serving. Makes 6 servings.

Nutrition information per serving: 264 calories, 4 g saturated fat, 2 g monounsaturated fat, 0 g polyunsaturated fat, 23 g protein, 26 g carbohydrate, 497 mg sodium, 327 mg potassium.

Before you start to assemble the lasagna, measure the noodles against the dish. If the noodles are longer than the dish, use scissors to trim them to fit. Start with a layer of noodles in the bottom of the dish. Then, top with layers of the cottage cheese mixture, the sauce, and the Parmesan cheese. Repeat these layers two more times.

Dijon Tofu Sandwiches

10 g fat
9 mg cholesterol

Our taste panel said the tofu spread for these hot sandwiches tasted like deviled eggs.

1 16-ounce package tofu, well drained
¼ cup shredded Monterey Jack cheese (1 ounce)
2 tablespoons reduced-calorie mayonnaise *or* salad dressing
4 teaspoons Dijon-style mustard
1 teaspoon garlic salt
4 bagels *or* English muffins, split and toasted

● In a medium mixing bowl use a fork to mash tofu. Stir in cheese, mayonnaise or salad dressing, mustard, and garlic salt; mix well. Spread tofu mixture on each bagel or English muffin half. Place on a baking sheet.

1 medium tomato, thinly sliced
1 cup alfalfa sprouts

● Broil 4 to 5 inches from the heat about 4 minutes or till light brown. Top with tomato and alfalfa sprouts. Makes 4 servings.

Nutrition information per serving: 319 calories, 3 g saturated fat, 2 g monounsaturated fat, 5 g polyunsaturated fat, 17 g protein, 39 g carbohydrate, 817 mg sodium, 256 mg potassium.

Lentil Stew

2 g fat
1 mg cholesterol

For added punch, use a can of Mexican- or Italian-style stewed tomatoes.

3 cups chicken broth
1 14½-ounce can stewed tomatoes
8 ounces (1¼ cups) dry lentils
1 large potato, peeled and chopped
1 medium carrot, chopped (½ cup)
1 medium onion, chopped (½ cup)
1 stalk celery, chopped (½ cup)
2 tablespoons snipped parsley
1 tablespoon dried basil, crushed
1 clove garlic, minced
Dash pepper

● In a large kettle or Dutch oven combine chicken broth, tomatoes, lentils, potato, carrot, onion, celery, parsley, basil, garlic, and pepper.

● Bring to boiling; reduce heat. Simmer, covered, for 35 to 40 minutes or till the lentils are tender. Makes 4 servings.

Nutrition information per serving: 289 calories, 0 g saturated fat, 1 g monounsaturated fat, 1 g polyunsaturated fat, 22 g protein, 49 g carbohydrate, 778 mg sodium, 1,176 mg potassium.

Side Dishes

*T*o add variety and round out your meal, choose from this tantalizing array of vegetable, pasta, rice, and bread recipes. Armed with dishes such as Wild Rice Dressing or Vegetable-Pasta Platter, you'll be reducing fat. Also, check out our special Oat Bran Baking Mix. It's a delicious way to add soluble fiber to your diet.

Side-Dish Pasta

Choose the flavor variation that best complements your entrée. (Lemon Pasta is pictured on the cover.)

4 ounces spaghetti, fettuccine, *or* linguine
2 teaspoons margarine *or* 1 teaspoon olive oil

● In a large saucepan bring a large amount of salted water to boiling. Add pasta; return to boiling. Reduce heat slightly. Cook till tender but still firm (8 to 10 minutes for fettuccine and linguine; 10 to 12 minutes for spaghetti). Drain well. Toss with margarine or olive oil. Serves 4.

Nutrition information per serving: 112 calories, 0 g saturated fat, 1 g monounsaturated fat, 1 g polyunsaturated fat, 3 g protein, 20 g carbohydrate, 23 mg sodium, 46 mg potassium.

Herbed Pasta
¾ teaspoon snipped fresh thyme, rosemary, *or* basil *or* ¼ teaspoon dried thyme, rosemary, *or* basil, crushed

Prepare Side-Dish Pasta as above, *except* add thyme, rosemary, *or* basil with the margarine or olive oil.

Nutrition information per serving: 112 calories, 2 g total fat (0 g saturated fat, 1 g monounsaturated fat, 1 g polyunsaturated fat), 0 mg cholesterol, 3 g protein, 20 g carbohydrate, 23 mg sodium, 46 mg potassium.

Dilled Pasta
1½ teaspoons snipped fresh dillweed *or* ½ teaspoon dried dillweed

Prepare Side-Dish Pasta as above, *except* add dillweed with the margarine or olive oil.

Nutrition information per serving: 112 calories, 2 g total fat (0 g saturated fat, 1 g monounsaturated fat, 1 g polyunsaturated fat), 0 mg cholesterol, 3 g protein, 20 g carbohydrate, 23 mg sodium, 46 mg potassium.

Lemon Pasta
2 tablespoons snipped parsley
½ teaspoon finely shredded lemon peel
⅛ teaspoon pepper

Prepare Side-Dish Pasta as above, *except* add parsley, lemon peel, and pepper with the margarine or olive oil.

Nutrition information per serving: 113 calories, 2 g total fat (0 g saturated fat, 1 g monounsaturated fat, 1 g polyunsaturated fat), 0 mg cholesterol, 3 g protein, 20 g carbohydrate, 23 mg sodium, 46 mg potassium.

Vegetable-Pasta Platter

2 g fat
7 mg cholesterol

Toss linguine and mixed vegetables with a rich Swiss cheese sauce.

3 ounces linguine *or* fettuccine

● In a large saucepan cook pasta in a large amount of boiling water for 8 minutes.

½ of a 16-ounce package (2½ cups) loose-pack frozen cauliflower, baby carrots, and pea pods

● Add vegetables. Return to boiling and cook for 1 to 2 minutes more or till pasta is just tender. Drain. Return to the saucepan. Cover to keep warm.

⅔ cup skim milk
1 tablespoon all-purpose flour
¼ teaspoon dried thyme, crushed
⅛ to ¼ teaspoon lemon-pepper seasoning
⅛ teaspoon salt
¼ cup shredded process Swiss cheese (2 ounces)

● Meanwhile, for sauce, in a small saucepan combine milk, flour, thyme, lemon-pepper seasoning, and salt. Cook and stir over medium heat till thickened and bubbly. Cook and stir 1 minute more. Stir in cheese till melted.

● Transfer pasta and vegetables to a warm serving platter. Pour sauce over vegetables and pasta. Toss gently to coat. Serve immediately. Makes 4 servings.

Nutrition information per serving: 146 calories, 1 g saturated fat, 0 g monounsaturated fat, 0 g polyunsaturated fat, 8 g protein, 24 g carbohydrate, 221 mg sodium, 331 mg potassium.

Spanish Rice

0 g fat
0 mg cholesterol

1 16-ounce can stewed tomatoes
1¼ cups water
⅔ cup long grain rice
½ cup chopped onion
1 clove garlic, minced
2 teaspoons chili powder
½ teaspoon salt
⅛ teaspoon pepper

● In a medium saucepan stir together the tomatoes, water, rice, onion, garlic, chili powder, salt, and pepper.

Bring to boiling; reduce heat. Simmer, covered, about 30 minutes or till rice is tender and most of the liquid is absorbed. Remove from the heat. Let stand for 10 minutes. Before serving, fluff with a fork. Makes 4 to 6 servings.

Nutrition information per serving: 155 calories, 0 g saturated fat, 0 g monounsaturated fat, 0 g polyunsaturated fat, 3 g protein, 35 g carbohydrate, 587 mg sodium, 87 mg potassium.

Curried Rice

0 g fat
0 mg cholesterol

Complement baked chicken or broiled fish with this flavor-packed side dish.

1½ **cups water**
⅔ **cup long grain rice**
¼ **cup raisins**
1 **to 2 teaspoons curry powder**
1½ **teaspoons instant chicken bouillon granules**
1 **teaspoon instant minced onion**

● In a medium saucepan stir together the water, rice, raisins, curry powder, bouillon granules, and minced onion. Bring to boiling; reduce heat. Simmer, covered, for 15 to 20 minutes or till rice is tender and liquid is absorbed.

   Remove from the heat. Let stand for 10 minutes. Before serving, fluff with a fork. Makes 4 servings.

Nutrition information per serving: 145 calories, 0 g saturated fat, 0 g monounsaturated fat, 0 g polyunsaturated fat, 3 g protein, 33 g carbohydrate, 340 mg sodium, 109 mg potassium.

Wild Rice Dressing

1 g fat
0 mg cholesterol

Water chestnuts lend a pleasant crunch.

¼ **cup wild rice**

● Rinse wild rice in a strainer under cold running water for 1 minute.

1¼ **cups water**
½ **cup chopped onion**
¼ **cup brown rice**
1½ **teaspoons instant chicken bouillon granules**
½ **teaspoon dried thyme, crushed**
⅛ **teaspoon pepper**

● In a medium saucepan combine wild rice, water, onion, brown rice, bouillon granules, thyme, and pepper. Bring to boiling; reduce heat. Simmer, covered, for 45 minutes.

2 **cups sliced fresh mushrooms**
½ **cup chopped celery**
½ **cup chopped water chestnuts**

● Stir mushrooms, celery, and water chestnuts into rice mixture. Return to boiling; reduce heat. Simmer, covered, for 10 to 20 minutes more or till celery is just tender, stirring occasionally. Makes 4 servings.

Nutrition information per serving: 108 calories, 0 g saturated fat, 0 g monounsaturated fat, 0 g polyunsaturated fat, 4 g protein, 23 g carbohydrate, 355 mg sodium, 272 mg potassium.

Zucchini Muffins

Oat Bran
Muffins

Apple Spirals

86

Oat Bran Baking Mix

2 g fat
1 mg cholesterol

Use this versatile mix to make the muffins, pancakes, and other breakfast breads found on the following pages.

2 cups all-purpose flour
2 cups whole wheat flour
2 cups whole bran cereal
1 cup oat bran
½ cup nonfat dry milk powder
½ cup packed brown sugar
3 tablespoons baking powder
1 teaspoon salt

● In a large mixing bowl stir together all-purpose flour, whole wheat flour, bran cereal, oat bran, nonfat dry milk powder, brown sugar, baking powder, and salt.

● To store, transfer mix to a tightly covered container. Makes 8 cups of mix.

Nutrition information per 1 cup: 366 calories, 0 g saturated fat, 1 g polyunsaturated fat, 0 g monounsaturated fat, 14 g protein, 86 g carbohydrate, 869 mg sodium, 594 mg potassium.

Oat Bran Pancakes

Oat Bran Muffins

4 grams fat
0 mg cholesterol

A basic muffin that tastes great with honey. (Pictured on pages 86–87.)

1 cup Oat Bran Baking Mix
   (see recipe, page 87)
1 slightly beaten egg white
¼ cup water
1 tablespoon cooking oil

● In a medium mixing bowl stir the Oat Bran Baking Mix. Stir together egg white, water, and cooking oil. Add to the baking mix all at once. Mix just till moistened. Line 4 muffin cups with paper bake cups or spray with nonstick spray coating. Spoon batter into muffin cups.

● Bake in a 400° oven about 20 minutes or till light brown. Serve warm. Makes 4.

Nutrition information per muffin: 126 calories, 1 g saturated fat, 2 g polyunsaturated fat, 1 g monounsaturated fat, 4 g protein, 22 g carbohydrate, 230 mg sodium, 160 mg potassium.

Zucchini Muffins

4 g fat
0 mg cholesterol

You can easily double the recipe to make eight muffins. (Pictured on pages 86–87.)

1 cup Oat Bran Baking Mix
   (see recipe, page 87)
1 slightly beaten egg white
3 tablespoons water
1 tablespoon cooking oil
1 tablespoon honey
½ teaspoon pumpkin pie spice
½ cup shredded zucchini

● In a large mixing bowl stir the Oat Bran Baking Mix. Stir together egg white, water, cooking oil, honey, and pumpkin pie spice. Add egg white mixture to the baking mix all at once. Mix just till moistened. Fold in zucchini. Line 4 muffin cups with paper bake cups or spray with nonstick spray coating. Spoon batter into muffin cups.

● Bake in a 400° oven about 18 minutes or till light brown. Serve warm. Makes 4.

Nutrition information per muffin: 145 calories, 1 g saturated fat, 2 g polyunsaturated fat, 1 g monounsaturated fat, 5 g protein, 27 g carbohydrate, 230 mg sodium, 204 mg potassium.

Apple Spirals

3 g fat
0 mg cholesterol

Brown sugar and ginger flavor the apple filling. (Pictured on pages 86–87.)

3 tablespoons margarine
2 cups Oat Bran Baking Mix
   (see recipe, page 87)
⅔ cup water

● In a medium mixing bowl cut margarine into Oat Bran Baking Mix till mixture resembles coarse crumbs. Add water all at once. Stir just till dough clings together. Let dough rest while preparing the filling.

⅔ cup finely chopped, peeled apple
   (1 small)
2 tablespoons brown sugar *or* sugar
⅛ teaspoon ground ginger
2 tablespoons skim milk

● For the filling, stir together apple, sugar, and ginger; set aside.
   On a well-floured surface knead the dough gently for 10 to 12 strokes (dough will be slightly sticky). Roll dough into a 12x8-inch rectangle. Brush with the skim milk. Sprinkle the filling over dough. Roll up jelly-roll style, starting from one of the long sides. Cut into 12 slices.

Nonstick spray coating
Powdered Sugar Glaze

● Spray a 9-inch round baking pan with nonstick coating. Arrange the slices, spiral-side up, in the pan. Bake in a 400° oven for 18 to 20 minutes or till golden. Drizzle warm rolls with Powdered Sugar Glaze. Makes 12.

Nutrition information per roll: 116 calories, 1 g saturated fat, 1 g polyunsaturated fat, 1 g monounsaturated fat, 2 g protein, 22 g carbohydrate, 181 mg sodium, 120 mg potassium.

Powdered Sugar Glaze
½ cup sifted powdered sugar
1 to 2 tablespoons skim milk

Combine powdered sugar and enough of the milk to make a glaze of drizzling consistency.

Buying Oat Bran

When buying oat bran for *Oat Bran Baking Mix* and other recipes in this book, be sure to choose 100 percent oat bran. This product looks like a coarse powder or flour, though it's really the outer hulls of whole oats that have been ground into tiny particles.
   In most grocery stores, you'll find it with the oatmeal and other hot cereals. Health food stores also sell oat bran. Just be sure not to substitute oat bran cereal flakes or other ready-to-eat oat bran cereals for 100 percent oat bran.

Oat Bran Pancakes

0 g fat
0 mg cholesterol

Our whole-grain pancakes are virtually fat-free. (Pictured on pages 86–87.)

2 slightly beaten egg whites
1⅓ cups water
2 cups Oat Bran Baking Mix
    (see recipe, page 87)

● In a medium mixing bowl combine egg whites and water. Add Oat Bran Baking Mix. Beat with a rotary beater till well blended.

Nonstick spray coating
Sliced nectarines, raspberries,
    ***and/or* blueberries (optional)**
Sifted powdered sugar (optional)

● Spray a *cold* griddle or heavy skillet with nonstick coating. Preheat griddle. Pour about ¼ *cup* batter onto griddle for *each* pancake. Cook over medium-high heat for 2 to 3 minutes or till light brown on both sides, turning once. If desired, serve with fresh fruit and sprinkle with powdered sugar. Makes 12 pancakes.

Nutrition information per pancake: 64 calories, 0 g saturated fat, 0 g polyunsaturated fat, 0 g monounsaturated fat, 3 g protein, 14 g carbohydrate, 153 mg sodium, 106 mg potassium.

Oat Bran Scones

3 g fat
0 mg cholesterol

A sugar-and-cinnamon topping sweetens these fruit-studded scones.

1⅓ cups Oat Bran Baking Mix
    (see recipe, page 87)
½ teaspoon ground cinnamon
2 tablespoons margarine

● In a medium bowl stir together Oat Bran Baking Mix and cinnamon. Cut in margarine till mixture resembles coarse crumbs.

⅓ cup dried currants, raisins,
    ***or* snipped pitted dates**
⅓ cup water
2 teaspoons sugar
¼ teaspoon ground cinnamon

● Stir in currants, raisins, or dates. Add water all at once. Stir just till dough clings together. On a lightly floured surface knead dough gently for 10 to 12 strokes. Roll or pat dough into a 7-inch circle. Cut into 8 wedges. Place wedges on an ungreased baking sheet. Stir together sugar and cinnamon. Sprinkle over wedges.
    Bake in a 450° oven for 8 to 10 minutes or till light brown. Makes 8.

Nutrition information per scone: 108 calories, 1 g saturated fat, 1 g monounsaturated fat, 1 g polyunsaturated fat, 3 g protein, 20 g carbohydrate, 178 mg sodium, 154 mg potassium.

Oat Bran Jelly Biscuits

4 g fat
1 mg cholesterol

2 **tablespoons margarine**
1¾ **cups Oat Bran Baking Mix**
(see recipe, page 87)
½ **cup skim milk**
6 **teaspoons jelly *or* jam**

● In a medium mixing bowl cut margarine into Oat Bran Baking Mix till mixture resembles coarse crumbs. Add skim milk all at once. Stir just till dough clings together.

On a lightly floured surface roll or pat dough to ½-inch thickness. Cut with a 2¼- to 2½-inch round biscuit cutter. Place on an ungreased baking sheet. Press your finger into the center of each biscuit to make an indentation. Spoon *1 teaspoon* jelly or jam into *each* center.

● Bake in a 450° oven about 8 minutes or till light brown. Serve warm. Makes 6 biscuits.

Nutrition information per biscuit: 164 calories, 1 g saturated fat, 1 g polyunsaturated fat, 2 g monounsaturated fat, 5 g protein, 30 g carbohydrate, 310 mg sodium, 214 mg potassium.

Nutmeg Coffee Cake

7 g fat
0 mg cholesterol

Nonstick spray coating
¾ **cup mixed dried fruit bits *or* raisins**
⅔ **cup skim milk**
2 **cups Oat Bran Baking Mix**
(see recipe, page 87)
1 **teaspoon finely shredded orange peel**
¼ **teaspoon ground nutmeg**

● Spray an 8x8x2-inch baking pan with nonstick coating; set aside. In a small bowl combine dried fruit and milk. Let stand for 10 minutes. Meanwhile, in a medium mixing bowl stir together Oat Bran Baking Mix, orange peel, and nutmeg.

2 **slightly beaten egg whites**
¼ **cup cooking oil**
2 **tablespoons honey**

● In a large bowl mix egg whites, oil, honey, and the fruit mixture. Stir baking mix mixture into egg white mixture. Pour batter into pan.

Orange Glaze

● Bake in a 350° oven 30 to 35 minutes or till a wooden toothpick inserted in center comes out clean. Cool on rack for 10 minutes. Drizzle with Orange Glaze. Serve warm. Serves 9.

Nutrition information per serving: 216 calories, 1 g saturated fat, 2 g monounsaturated fat, 4 g polyunsaturated fat, 5 g protein, 38 g carbohydrate, 222 mg sodium, 271 mg potassium.

Orange Glaze
½ **cup sifted powdered sugar**
¼ **teaspoon finely shredded orange peel**
2 **to 3 teaspoons orange juice**

In a mixing bowl stir together powdered sugar, orange peel, and *2 teaspoons* orange juice. Stir till smooth. Add additional orange juice to make a glaze of drizzling consistency.

91

Oven Fries

6 g fat
5 mg cholesterol

Satisfy your yen for french fries with this low-fat version.

**4 small baking potatoes
(about 1 pound total)
1 tablespoon margarine, melted**

● Scrub potatoes thoroughly. Cut *each* potato lengthwise into *8* slices. Brush cut surface of potatoes lightly with melted margarine.

**¼ cup grated Parmesan cheese
½ teaspoon garlic salt
¼ teaspoon paprika
⅛ teaspoon onion powder (optional)
Nonstick spray coating**

● In a plastic bag combine Parmesan cheese, garlic salt, paprika, and, if desired, onion powder. Add *8* potato slices to bag. Shake to coat (potatoes will not be completely coated). Spray an 11x7x1½-inch baking pan with nonstick coating. Arrange potatoes in baking pan. Repeat with remaining potatoes.
　　Bake, uncovered, in a 400° oven for 25 to 30 minutes or till tender. Serve hot. Makes 3 or 4 servings.

Nutrition information per serving: 233 calories, 2 g saturated fat, 2 g monounsaturated fat, 1 g polyunsaturated fat, 6 g protein, 39 g carbohydrate, 360 mg sodium, 649 mg potassium.

 Microwave Directions: Cut potatoes and coat with Parmesan mixture as directed above. Arrange in a 12x7½x2-inch microwave-safe baking dish. Cover with vented plastic wrap. Micro-cook on 100% power (high) for 9 to 11 minutes or till almost tender, rotating dish once. Let stand 2 to 3 minutes before serving.

Scalloped Potatoes

1 g fat
3 mg cholesterol

**1 cup skim milk
2 teaspoons cornstarch
¼ teaspoon salt
¼ teaspoon pepper**

● For sauce, in a small saucepan stir together the milk, cornstarch, salt, and pepper. Cook and stir over medium heat till thickened and bubbly. Remove from the heat. Set aside.

**Nonstick spray coating
2 large potatoes
¼ cup chopped onion**

● Lightly spray the sides of a 1½-quart casserole with nonstick coating. Peel potatoes and slice very thin. Layer *half* of the potatoes and *half* of the onion into the casserole. Repeat layers of potatoes and onion.

2 tablespoons grated Parmesan cheese

● Pour sauce over potato mixture. Sprinkle with Parmesan cheese. Bake, covered, in a 350° oven for 40 minutes.
　　Uncover and bake for 10 to 15 minutes more or till potatoes are tender. Serves 4.

Nutrition information per serving: 134 calories, 1 g saturated fat, 0 g monounsaturated fat, 0 g polyunsaturated fat, 5 g protein, 26 g carbohydrate, 217 mg sodium, 503 mg potassium.

Skillet Squash

0 g fat
0 mg cholesterol

Simmering acorn squash rings takes only half the time of regular baking.

**1 medium acorn squash
  (about 1 pound)**

● Cut squash crosswise into ½- to ¾-inch slices; discard seeds. Arrange in a large skillet.

**⅓ cup pineapple-orange juice
1 tablespoon brown sugar
¼ teaspoon gound nutmeg
  Dash salt**

● In a small bowl combine juice, sugar, nutmeg, and salt. Pour over squash rings. Bring to boiling; reduce heat. Simmer, covered, for 20 to 25 minutes or till squash is tender.
  Arrange squash rings on a platter. Pour sauce over squash. Makes 3 or 4 servings.

Nutrition information per serving: 101 calories, 0 g saturated fat, 0 g monounsaturated fat, 0 g polyunsaturated fat, 2 g protein, 26 g carbohydrate, 50 mg sodium, 599 mg potassium.

Microwave Directions: Cut squash and remove seeds as directed above. Arrange in a 12x7½x2-inch microwave-safe baking dish. In a small bowl combine juice, brown sugar, nutmeg, and salt. Pour over squash rings. Cover with vented microwave-safe plastic wrap. Micro-cook on 100% power (high) for 11 to 13 minutes or till squash is tender, turning and rearranging squash once. Serve as above. (Not recommended for low-wattage ovens.)

Use a heavy knife to cut the acorn squash crosswise into ½- to ¾-inch slices. Then, scrape out the seeds with a spoon.

Creamed Vegetables

3 g fat
1 mg cholesterol

2 medium potatoes, peeled and cubed
¾ cup frozen peas and carrots
¼ cup water

● In a medium saucepan stir together potatoes, peas and carrots, and water. Bring to boiling; reduce heat. Simmer, covered, for 15 to 20 minutes or till tender. Drain; return vegetables to the saucepan. Cover to keep warm.

¼ cup chopped green *or* sweet
    red pepper
2 tablespoons sliced green onion
1 tablespoon margarine
1 tablespoon all-purpose flour
¼ teaspoon salt
¼ teaspoon dried dillweed
⅛ teaspoon pepper
¾ cup skim milk

● For sauce, in a small saucepan cook green or sweet red pepper and onion in margarine till tender. Stir in flour, salt, dillweed, and pepper. Add milk all at once. Cook and stir over medium heat till thickened and bubbly. Cook and stir for 1 minute more. Stir sauce into the vegetable mixture in the saucepan. Heat through. Makes 4 servings.

Nutrition information per serving: 124 calories, 1 g saturated fat, 1 g monounsaturated fat, 1 g polyunsaturated fat, 4 g protein, 21 g carbohydrate, 215 mg sodium, 371 mg potassium.

Italian Zucchini

1 g fat
2 mg cholesterol

Savor the flavors of Parmesan cheese, thyme, and garlic with zucchini and tomatoes.

2 small zucchini, sliced ¼ inch thick
    (1½ to 2 cups)
1 small onion, sliced and separated
    into rings (⅓ cup)
2 cups cherry tomatoes, halved

● Place steamer basket in a large saucepan. Add water to just below the basket. Bring to boiling. Place zucchini and onion in steamer basket. Cover and steam for 5 minutes. Add tomatoes. Cook, covered, about 2 minutes more or till tomatoes are just heated through.

2 tablespoons grated Parmesan cheese
¼ teaspoon dried thyme, crushed
⅛ teaspoon garlic powder

● Meanwhile, in a small bowl stir together Parmesan cheese, thyme, and garlic powder.

● Carefully remove steamer basket from saucepan. Transfer vegetables to a serving bowl. Sprinkle Parmesan cheese mixture over vegetables. Toss gently. Makes 4 servings.

Nutrition information per serving: 36 calories, 1 g saturated fat, 0 g monounsaturated fat, 0 g polyunsaturated fat, 2 g protein, 5 g carbohydrate, 54 mg sodium, 273 mg potassium.

 Microwave Directions: Place zucchini and onion in a 1½-quart microwave-safe casserole. Add 2 tablespoons *water*. Micro-cook, covered, on 100% power (high) for 3 to 4 minutes or till almost tender.

Drain; return vegetables to the casserole. Stir in tomatoes. Cook, covered, on high for 2 to 2½ minutes or till tomatoes are just heated through. Stir together cheese, thyme, and garlic powder. Sprinkle over vegetables. Toss gently.

Asparagus and Tomatoes

0 g fat
0 mg cholesterol

½ **pound asparagus** *or* **one 10-ounce package frozen cut asparagus** ¼ **cup chopped onion**	● Snap off and discard woody bases from fresh asparagus. Scrape off scales, if desired. Bias-slice into 2-inch pieces. In a medium saucepan cook asparagus and onion, covered, in a small amount of boiling salted water for 5 to 7 minutes or till just tender. (*Or,* cook frozen asparagus and onion according to asparagus package directions.) Drain; return to saucepan.
1 **tablespoon soy sauce** ¼ **teaspoon dried oregano, crushed** ⅛ **teaspoon salt** ⅛ **teaspoon garlic powder**	● In a custard cup stir together soy sauce, oregano, salt, and garlic powder. Add to asparagus mixture and stir to coat.
2 **small tomatoes, cut into wedges and seeded** ½ **cup sliced water chestnuts**	● Stir tomatoes and water chestnuts into asparagus mixture. Cover and cook about 1 minute or till heated through. Serve immediately. Makes 4 servings.

Nutrition information per serving: 40 calories, 0 g saturated fat, 0 g monounsaturated fat, 0 g polyunsaturated fat, 3 g protein, 8 g carbohydrate, 331 mg sodium, 344 mg potassium.

Garden Soup

1 g fat
4 mg cholesterol

Chock-full of fresh vegetables.

2 **cups asparagus bias-sliced 1-inch thick** *or* **chopped broccoli** ½ **cup sliced carrot** ½ **cup water** ¼ **cup sliced green onion** ½ **teaspoon salt** ½ **teaspoon fines herbes** **Dash pepper**	● In a large saucepan stir together asparagus or broccoli, carrot, water, onion, salt, fines herbes, and pepper. Bring to boiling; reduce heat. Simmer, covered, for 5 minutes.
½ **cup sliced zucchini, halved**	● Stir in zucchini. Cook, covered, about 2 minutes more or till just tender.
1 **12-ounce can evaporated skim milk** 4 **teaspoons cornstarch** 1 **cup skim milk**	● Stir together *2 tablespoons* of the evaporated milk and the cornstarch. Stir into vegetable mixture. Stir in remaining evaporated milk and skim milk. Cook and stir till thickened and bubbly. Cook and stir 2 minutes more. Serves 4.

Nutrition information per serving: 135 calories, 0 g saturated fat, 0 g monounsaturated fat, 0 g polyunsaturated fat, 11 g protein, 22 g carbohydrate, 414 mg sodium, 781 mg potassium.

Pasta Salad

3 g fat
0 mg cholesterol

Create a different salad each time just by varying the salad dressing for the marinade.

1½ **cups cooked corkscrew macaroni**
   or **spaghetti (about 3 ounces uncooked pasta)**
⅓ **cup reduced-calorie creamy cucumber, French, *or* Italian salad dressing**

● In a colander rinse cooked macaroni or spaghetti with *cold* water; drain well. In a large bowl combine the pasta and salad dressing. Toss to coat.

½ **medium cucumber, quartered lengthwise and sliced**
½ **cup chopped green pepper**
1 **small onion, chopped (⅓ cup)**
2 **tablespoons snipped parsley**

● Add the cucumber, green pepper, onion, and snipped parsley to the pasta mixture. Toss gently. Cover and chill for 4 to 24 hours.

1 **cup cherry tomatoes, halved**

● Before serving, stir in the cherry tomatoes. Makes 4 servings.

Nutrition information per serving: 153 calories, 0 g saturated fat, 0 g monounsaturated fat, 1 g polyunsaturated fat, 4 g protein, 27 g carbohydrate, 400 mg sodium, 177 mg potassium.

Cauliflower Salad

6 g fat
5 mg cholesterol

Parmesan cheese dressing accents the garbanzo beans and cauliflower.

3 **cups cauliflower flowerets**
1 **15-ounce can garbanzo beans, drained**
1 **cup sliced celery**
1 **small onion, chopped**

● In a medium bowl combine the cauliflower, garbanzo beans, celery, and chopped onion.

⅓ **cup plain low-fat yogurt**
¼ **cup reduced-calorie mayonnaise** *or* **salad dressing**
2 **tablespoons grated Parmesan cheese**
1 **teaspoon sugar**

● In a small bowl combine yogurt, mayonnaise or salad dressing, Parmesan cheese, and sugar. Mix well. Pour over cauliflower mixture and toss gently. Cover and chill for 3 to 24 hours.

Spinach leaves

● Before serving, arrange spinach on 6 salad plates or in a shallow serving dish. Top with cauliflower mixture. Makes 6 servings.

Nutrition information per serving: 180 calories, 1 g saturated fat, 1 g monounsaturated fat, 3 g polyunsaturated fat, 9 g protein, 25 g carbohydrate, 140 mg sodium, 524 mg potassium.

Pasta Salad

Mixed Vegetable Salad

0 g fat
0 mg cholesterol

To shortcut the preparation time, just thaw and substitute a 16-ounce package of frozen broccoli, cauliflower, and carrots for the fresh vegetables.

2 tablespoons sugar
2 teaspoons all-purpose flour
½ teaspoon dry mustard
¼ teaspoon salt
⅛ teaspoon pepper

● For the dressing, in a small saucepan stir together the sugar, all-purpose flour, dry mustard, salt, and pepper.

¼ cup red wine vinegar
¼ cup water

● Add the vinegar and water to the saucepan. Cook and stir over medium heat till mixture is thickened and bubbly. Cook and stir for 1 minute more. Cool.

2 cups broccoli flowerets
2 cups cauliflower flowerets
1 small onion, chopped
2 tablespoons sliced pimiento, drained

● In a medium bowl combine the broccoli, cauliflower, onion, and pimiento. Pour dressing over vegetables. Toss to coat. Cover and chill for 4 to 24 hours. Makes 4 servings.

Nutrition information per serving: 63 calories, 0 g saturated fat, 0 g monounsaturated fat, 0 g polyunsaturated fat, 3 g protein, 14 g carbohydrate, 153 mg sodium, 362 mg potassium.

Spinach-Orange Salad

0 g fat
0 mg cholesterol

Oil-Free Salad Dressing is delicious with spinach or other salad greens.

3 cups torn spinach
3 cups torn lettuce
1 11-ounce can mandarin orange
**   sections, drained**
1 small red onion, thinly sliced
Oil-Free Salad Dressing

● In a salad bowl combine spinach, lettuce, orange sections, and onion. Add the Oil-Free Salad Dressing. Toss to coat. Makes 6 servings.

Nutrition information per serving: 54 calories, 0 g saturated fat, 0 g monounsaturated fat, 0 g polyunsaturated fat, 1 g protein, 13 g carbohydrate, 28 mg sodium, 261 mg potassium.

Oil-Free Salad Dressing
1 tablespoon powdered fruit pectin
½ teaspoon sugar
¼ teaspoon dried basil, crushed
⅛ teaspoon dry mustard
⅛ teaspoon garlic powder
¼ cup water
1 tablespoon red wine vinegar

Combine pectin, sugar, basil, mustard, and garlic powder. Stir in water and vinegar. Cover and chill at least 1 hour before using. Store any remaining dressing in the refrigerator for up to 3 days. Makes 6 (4-teaspoon) servings.

Nutrition information per serving: 9 calories, 0 g total fat (0 g saturated fat, 0 g monounsaturated fat, 0 g polyunsaturated fat), 0 mg cholesterol, 0 g protein, 2 g carbohydrate, 0 mg sodium, 6 mg potassium.

Curried Bean Salad

1 g fat
0 mg cholesterol

Surprise your taste buds with a delicious blend of French salad dressing and curry.

1 8½-ounce can lima beans
1 8-ounce can wax *or* green beans
1 8-ounce can red kidney beans
½ cup chopped green pepper
¼ cup sliced green onion

● Drain the lima beans, wax or green beans, and kidney beans.
   In a medium bowl stir together the lima beans, wax or green beans, kidney beans, green pepper, and green onion.

¼ cup reduced-calorie French salad
    dressing
¼ teaspoon curry powder

● In a small bowl stir together French dressing and curry powder. Add to bean mixture; toss gently. Cover; chill for 4 to 24 hours. Serves 6.

Nutrition information per serving: 92 calories, 0 g saturated fat, 0 g monounsaturated fat, 1 g polyunsaturated fat, 5 g protein, 16 g carbohydrate, 510 mg sodium, 247 mg potassium.

Fruit Bowl

1 g fat
1 mg cholesterol

1 tablespoon sugar
1 tablespoon cornstarch
1 8-ounce can crushed pineapple
    (juice pack)
⅓ cup plain low-fat yogurt

● For dressing, in a small saucepan combine sugar and cornstarch. Add *undrained* pineapple. Cook and stir till thickened and bubbly. Cook and stir for 2 minutes more. Remove from heat. Stir yogurt into dressing till well blended. Cover and chill for 2 to 24 hours.

4 cups cut-up fresh fruit (strawberries,
    grapes, apples, pears, *and/or*
    oranges)

● Before serving, add dressing to fresh fruit; toss gently. Makes 5 servings.

Nutrition information per serving: 114 calories, 0 g saturated fat, 0 g monounsaturated fat, 0 g polyunsaturated fat, 2 g protein, 27 g carbohydrate, 12 mg sodium, 289 mg potassium.

Citrus Coleslaw

0 g fat
1 mg cholesterol

Spike fruit-flavored yogurt with a touch of ginger for a light, refreshing dressing.

½ cup orange *or* lemon low-fat yogurt
1 tablespoon skim milk
⅛ teaspoon ground ginger
3 cups shredded coleslaw mix *or* 3
    cups of shredded cabbage and
    grated carrot
1 11-ounce can mandarin orange
    sections, chilled and drained, *or* 1
    cup fresh orange sections, drained

● In a medium mixing bowl combine yogurt, milk, and ginger. Stir together well.
   Add coleslaw mix and orange sections to yogurt mixture; toss to coat. Serves 4.

Nutrition information per serving: 94 calories, 0 g saturated fat, 0 g polyunsaturated fat, 0 g monounsaturated fat, 2 g protein, 22 g carbohydrate, 35 mg sodium, 275 mg potassium.

99

Kidney Bean Salad

6 g fat
5 mg cholesterol

Crunchy jicama replaces the traditional hard-cooked eggs for a low-cholesterol salad.

1 **15½-ounce can red kidney beans, drained** 4 **ounces jicama, peeled and cut into thin 1-inch strips (½ cup)** 2 **green onions, sliced**	● In a medium mixing bowl stir together the kidney beans, jicama, and onions.
¼ **cup reduced-calorie mayonnaise** *or* **salad dressing** 2 **tablespoons dill pickle relish** ¼ **teaspoon celery seed**	● In a small bowl stir together mayonnaise or salad dressing, pickle relish, and celery seed. Pour over bean mixture. Toss lightly to coat. Cover and chill for 3 to 24 hours.
Lettuce leaves	● Before serving, line 4 salad plates with lettuce leaves. Spoon bean mixture atop lettuce. Makes 4 servings.

Nutrition information per serving: 187 calories, 1 g saturated fat, 0 g monounsaturated fat, 3 g polyunsaturated fat, 8 g protein, 27 g carbohydrate, 160 mg sodium, 430 mg potassium.

Bean-Carrot Salad

2 g fat
0 mg cholesterol

Dill highlights the flavor of the marinated vegetables.

1 **9-ounce package frozen Italian-style green beans** ½ **cup water** 2 **medium carrots, bias sliced (1 cup)**	● In a medium saucepan combine beans and water. Bring to boiling; reduce heat. Simmer, covered, for 2 minutes. Stir in carrots. Cook, covered, about 5 minutes or till beans and carrots are crisp-tender. Drain.
½ **cup sliced celery**	● In a medium bowl combine beans, carrots, and celery.
3 **tablespoons vinegar** 2 **teaspoons salad oil** 1 **teaspoon sugar** ½ **teaspoon dried dillweed** ¼ **teaspoon salt** **Lettuce leaves (optional)**	● In a small bowl combine vinegar, oil, sugar, dillweed, and salt. Pour over carrot mixture. Toss gently. Cover and chill for 6 to 24 hours. Using a slotted spoon, serve mixture on lettuce, if desired. Makes 4 to 6 servings.

Nutrition information per serving: 69 calories, 0 g saturated fat, 1 g monounsaturated fat, 1 g polyunsaturated fat, 2 g protein, 12 g carbohydrate, 173 mg sodium, 286 mg potassium.

Baked Beans

3 g fat
8 mg cholesterol

Substituting ham for bacon gives lots of flavor and cuts the fat in half.

Nonstick spray coating
½ cup chopped onion
1 clove garlic, minced

● Spray a *cold* small skillet with nonstick coating. Preheat skillet, then add onion and garlic. Cook till onion is tender but not brown, stirring occasionally.

1 15½-ounce can red kidney beans, drained
1 8½-ounce can lima beans, drained
1 8-ounce can pork and beans with tomato sauce
½ cup diced lean fully cooked ham
⅓ cup catsup
1 tablespoon brown sugar
1 tablespoon Worcestershire sauce
2 to 3 teaspoons prepared mustard

● In a 1½-quart casserole combine the onion mixture and remaining ingredients. Bake, covered, in a 375° oven for 30 to 60 minutes or till desired consistency. Makes 6 servings.

Nutrition information per serving: 192 calories, 1 g saturated fat, 1 g monounsaturated fat, 1 g polyunsaturated fat, 10 g protein, 32 g carbohydrate, 880 mg sodium, 503 mg potassium.

 Microwave Directions: In a 1½-quart microwave-safe casserole, combine onion, garlic, and 1 tablespoon *water.* Micro-cook, covered, on 100% power (high) for 2 minutes. Drain. Stir together onion mixture and remaining ingredients. Cook, covered, on high for 6 to 8 minutes or till bubbly. Cook, uncovered, on 50% power (medium) for 10 minutes more, stirring twice.

Black-Eyed Peas

1 g fat
6 mg cholesterol

½ pound dry black-eyed peas (1¼ cups)
4 cups water

● Rinse peas. In a large saucepan combine the peas and water. Bring to boiling; reduce heat. Simmer, uncovered, for 2 minutes. Remove from heat. Cover and let stand for 1 hour. (*Or,* soak peas in water overnight.)

2½ cups water
½ cup diced lean fully cooked ham
1 small onion, chopped
1 tablespoon Worcestershire sauce
¼ teaspoon salt
¼ teaspoon bottled hot pepper sauce
⅛ teaspoon pepper

● Drain and rinse peas. Return to saucepan. Stir in water, ham, onion, Worcestershire sauce, salt, hot pepper sauce, and pepper. Bring to boiling; reduce heat. Simmer, covered, for 1 to 1¼ hours or till peas are tender.

Chopped tomatoes (optional)
Finely chopped celery (optional)
Sliced green onion (optional)

● Ladle into 6 sauce dishes. If desired, pass tomatoes, celery, and green onion to sprinkle atop black-eyed peas. Makes 6 servings.

Nutrition information per serving: 151 calories, 0 g saturated fat, 0 g monounsaturated fat, 0 g polyunsaturated fat, 12 g protein, 23 g carbohydrate, 279 mg sodium, 472 mg potassium.

101

Vegetable Fix-Ups

Make the vegetable the main attraction of the menu with an easy fix-up. Use the suggested vegetable or another favorite.

● **Oriental Vegetables:** In a medium saucepan cook one 16-ounce package loose-pack frozen *broccoli, carrots, water chestnuts, and red peppers* according to package directions. Drain.

Meanwhile, for sauce, in a small saucepan stir together ½ cup *water or chicken broth,* 1 tablespoon *soy sauce,* 1½ teaspoons *cornstarch,* ⅛ teaspoon ground *ginger,* and dash *garlic powder.* Cook and stir till thickened and bubbly. Cook and stir for 2 minutes more. Pour sauce over vegetables; toss to coat. Serves 4 to 6.

102

●**Beans with Salsa:** Heat one 15½-ounce can whole *wax or green beans. Or,* cook one 9-ounce package frozen cut *wax beans, green beans, Italian-style green beans, or baby lima beans* according to package directions.

Meanwhile, heat ½ cup *red salsa.* Drain beans and place in a serving bowl. Pour salsa over beans. Sprinkle with chopped *green or sweet red pepper,* if desired. Makes 4 servings.

●**Vegetables with Lemon-Mustard Sauce:** Cook two 10-ounce packages frozen *asparagus spears, broccoli spears, or cauliflower* according to package directions. Drain.

Meanwhile, in a small saucepan combine ⅔ cup *water,* 4 teaspoons *all-purpose flour,* 1 tablespoon *lemon juice,* 1 to 2 teaspoons *prepared mustard,* ½ teaspoon instant *chicken bouillon granules,* and ⅛ teaspoon *pepper.* Cook and stir till thickened and bubbly. Cook and stir 1 minute more. Serve over vegetables. Serves 6.

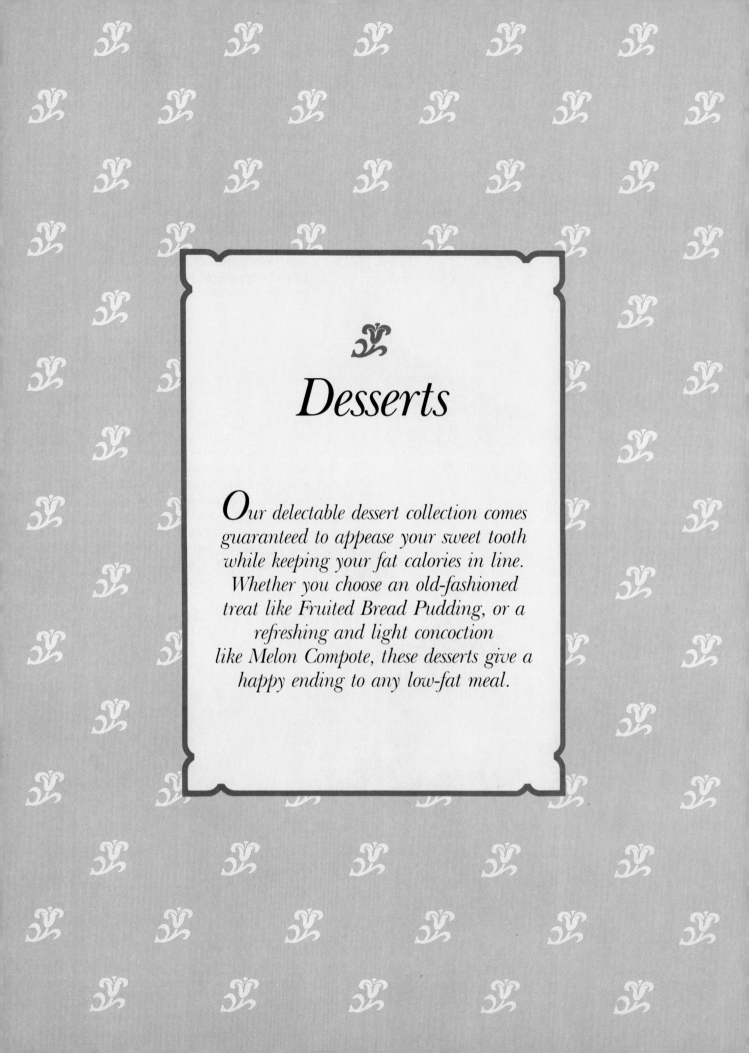

Desserts

*O*ur delectable dessert collection comes
guaranteed to appease your sweet tooth
while keeping your fat calories in line.
Whether you choose an old-fashioned
treat like Fruited Bread Pudding, or a
refreshing and light concoction
like Melon Compote, these desserts give a
happy ending to any low-fat meal.

Fruited Bread Pudding

1 g fat
25 mg cholesterol

A spectacular meringue topping, crushed pineapple, and your choice of dried fruit team up for an outstanding bread pudding.

Nonstick spray coating
3½ **cups toasted whole wheat *or* white bread cubes (about 5 slices)**
1 **8-ounce can crushed pineapple (juice pack), drained**
½ **cup chopped pitted dates, chopped dried cherries, raisins, *or* snipped dried apricots**

● Spray an 8x8x2-inch baking dish with nonstick coating. Spread *half* of the bread cubes over the bottom of the dish. Top with pineapple and dates, dried cherries, raisins, or dried apricots. Sprinkle remaining bread cubes over fruit layer.

2 **egg whites**
1 **egg**
1 **13-ounce can evaporated skim milk**
⅓ **cup sugar**
⅓ **cup water**
1½ **teaspoons vanilla**
½ **teaspoon ground cinnamon**

● In a medium mixing bowl beat together egg whites, whole egg, evaporated skim milk, sugar, water, vanilla, and cinnamon. Pour over fruit and bread.
   Bake in a 350° oven for 30 to 40 minutes or till a knife inserted near the center comes out clean. Remove pudding from oven. Increase oven temperature to 450°.

3 **egg whites**
¼ **teaspoon cream of tartar**
⅓ **cup sugar**

● Meanwhile, for meringue, in a large mixing bowl combine egg whites and cream of tartar. Beat with an electric mixer on medium speed till soft peaks form (tips curl). Gradually add sugar, 1 tablespoon at a time, beating till stiff peaks form (tips stand straight).

● Gently spread the meringue evenly over the hot pudding. Return to oven. Bake for 4 to 5 minutes more or till the meringue is golden. Makes 9 servings.

Nutrition information per serving: 182 calories, 0 g saturated fat, 1 g monounsaturated fat, 0 g polyunsaturated fat, 7 g protein, 37 g carbohydrate, 169 mg sodium, 269 mg potassium.

Ice Milk Shake

4 g fat
15 mg cholesterol

Indulge in this creamy shake made with ice milk and skim milk.

¾ **cup ice milk (any flavor)**
¼ **cup skim milk**

● In a blender container combine ice milk and skim milk. Cover; blend till smooth. Pour into a chilled glass. Serve immediately. Serves 1.

Nutrition information per serving: 159 calories, 3 g saturated fat, 1 g monounsaturated fat, 0 g polyunsaturated fat, 6 g protein, 25 g carbohydrate, 110 mg sodium, 300 mg potassium.

Glazed Peaches

4 g fat
5 mg cholesterol

Brown sugar and brandy make a sauce reminiscent of Bananas Foster.

**2 medium peaches *or* nectarines
   or 2 cups frozen unsweetened
   peach slices**

● Peel fresh peaches or nectarines, if desired. Pit and slice peaches or nectarines.

**¼ cup packed brown sugar
1 tablespoon water
1 tablespoon brandy *or* rum
1 tablespoon margarine
1 teaspoon lemon juice
¼ teaspoon ground mace *or*
   ⅛ teaspoon ground nutmeg**

● For sauce, in an 8-inch skillet stir together the brown sugar, water, brandy or rum, margarine, lemon juice, and mace or nutmeg. Bring to boiling, stirring occasionally.

● Add fresh peaches or nectarines or frozen peaches to the sauce; stir gently. Reduce heat. Simmer, covered, about 5 minutes for fresh peaches or about 10 minutes for frozen peaches or till tender.

1 cup vanilla ice milk

● Place a ¼-cup scoop of ice milk into *each* of 4 dessert dishes. Arrange peaches around ice milk; spoon sauce over top. Makes 4 servings.

Nutrition information per serving: 150 calories, 1 g saturated fat, 2 g monounsaturated fat, 1 g polyunsaturated fat, 2 g protein, 27 g carbohydrate, 66 mg sodium, 203 mg potassium.

Fruit Compote

0 g fat
0 mg cholesterol

Create a flavorful compote with fresh fruits of the season. (Pictured on the cover.)

**1 cup ginger ale
2 tablespoons frozen orange *or*
   pineapple juice concentrate**

● In a small bowl stir together the ginger ale and juice concentrate. Pour into an 8x4x2-inch loaf pan. Freeze at least 2½ hours or till firm.

**3 cups fresh fruit (cantaloupe balls,
   honeydew melon balls,
   strawberries, nectarine slices,
   and/or pitted cherries)
Mint sprigs (optional)**

● Divide fruit among 4 to 6 dessert dishes or champagne glasses. With a heavy spoon, scrape surface of ginger ale mixture and spoon it over fruit. Garnish with mint, if desired. Serve immediately. Makes 4 to 6 servings.

Nutrition information per serving: 75 calories, 0 g saturated fat, 0 g monounsaturated fat, 0 g polyunsaturated fat, 1 g protein, 19 g carbohydrate, 13 mg sodium, 361 mg potassium.

Glazed Peaches

Cherry Tortes
(see recipe, page 108)

Cherry Tortes

5 g fat
0 mg cholesterol

Assemble this dessert up to 12 hours ahead. (Pictured on page 107.)

2 egg whites	● Place egg whites in a medium mixing bowl. Let stand at room temperature 1 hour. Cover a baking sheet with plain brown paper. Draw six 3½-inch circles on the paper. Set aside.
½ teaspoon vanilla **¼ teaspoon cream of tartar** **Dash salt**	● Add vanilla, cream of tartar, and salt to egg whites. Beat with an electric mixer on medium speed till soft peaks form (tips curl).
¾ cup sugar **¼ cup unsweetened cocoa powder, sifted**	● Add sugar, *1 tablespoon* at a time, beating on high speed till stiff peaks form (tips stand straight) and sugar is almost dissolved. Beat in cocoa powder on low speed.
	● Divide beaten egg whites among the 6 circles on the brown paper. Using a spoon, spread the mixture over each circle building up the sides and forming a pocket. Bake in a 300° oven for 35 minutes. Turn off oven. Let shells dry in oven with door closed for 1 hour. Peel off paper. Store in an airtight container.
1 1.4-ounce envelope whipped dessert topping mix **½ cup skim milk** **1 21-ounce can cherry *or* red raspberry pie filling, chilled** **1 tablespoon lemon juice** **2 tablespoons toasted sliced almonds**	● To serve, prepare topping mix according to package directions, *except* use the skim milk. Stir together the chilled pie filling and lemon juice. Arrange meringue shells on 6 dessert plates. Top each with pie filling mixture and dessert topping. Sprinkle with almonds. Chill up to 12 hours. Makes 6 servings.

Nutrition information per serving: 267 calories, 3 g saturated fat, 1 g monounsaturated fat, 0 g polyunsaturated fat, 4 g protein, 57 g carbohydrate, 96 mg sodium, 208 mg potassium.

Chocolate Angel Cake

1 g fat
0 mg cholesterol

Stir cocoa powder into the cake mix and presto, you have a fantastic chocolate cake. (Pictured on page 110.)

1 package angel cake mix **⅓ cup unsweetened cocoa powder**	● Prepare cake mix according to package directions, *except* sift cocoa powder and stir into dry ingredients for a one-step mix or into flour ingredients for a two-step mix. Serves 12.

Nutrition information per serving: 131 calories, 0 g saturated fat, 0 g monounsaturated fat, 0 g polyunsaturated fat, 4 g protein, 30 g carbohydrate, 269 mg sodium, 99 mg potassium.

Peppermint Meringues

0 g fat
0 mg cholesterol

Pass a tray of these morsels for an after-dinner refresher.

2 egg whites

● Place egg whites in a medium mixing bowl and let stand at room temperature for 1 hour.

½ teaspoon vanilla
⅛ teaspoon cream of tartar
⅔ cup sugar

● Add vanilla and cream of tartar to egg whites. Beat with an electric mixer on medium speed till soft peaks form (tips curl).

Add sugar, *1 tablespoon* at a time, beating on high speed till stiff peaks form (tips stand straight) and sugar is almost dissolved.

¼ cup finely crushed striped round peppermint candies *or* hard cinnamon candies

● Grease cookie sheet; set aside. Gently fold crushed candies into beaten egg whites. Drop from a rounded teaspoon 1½ inches apart on prepared cookie sheet. Bake in a 325° oven for 10 to 12 minutes or till set and lightly browned on the edges. Turn off oven. Let dry in oven with door closed for 20 minutes. Remove from sheet. Store in an airtight container. Makes 30.

Nutrition information per meringue: 24 calories, 0 g saturated fat, 0 g monounsaturated fat, 0 g polyunsaturated fat, 0 g protein, 6 g carbohydrate, 5 mg sodium, 4 mg potassium.

Chocolate-Peppermint Meringues
2 tablespoons unsweetened cocoa powder

Prepare Peppermint Meringues as above, *except* use striped round peppermint candies (*do not* use other candies). Sift cocoa powder and stir into crushed candies. Fold into beaten egg whites. Continue as above.

Nutrition information per meringue: 25 calories, 0 g total fat (0 g saturated fat, 0 g monounsaturated fat, 0 g polyunsaturated fat), 0 mg cholesterol, 0 g protein, 6 g carbohydrate, 5 mg sodium, 8 mg potassium.

When egg whites are stiffly beaten, the tips will stand straight up and not curl over after the beaters are lifted out of the mixture.

Chocolate Angel Cake
(see recipe, page 108)

Berry Sauce

Chocolate Sauce

Fruit Sauce

Chocolate Sauce

1 g fat
0 mg cholesterol

Serve any of the delicious sauces on this page over angel cake, ice milk, or frozen yogurt.

¾ **cup sugar**
⅓ **cup unsweetened cocoa powder**
4 **teaspoons cornstarch**
⅔ **cup evaporated skim milk**
1 **teaspoon vanilla**

● In small saucepan mix sugar, cocoa powder, and cornstarch. Add milk. Cook and stir till thickened and bubbly. Cook and stir 2 minutes more. Remove from heat. Stir in vanilla. Serve warm or cool. Refrigerate any remaining sauce. Makes 8 (2-tablespoon) servings.

Nutrition information per serving: 94 calories, 0 g saturated fat, 0 g monounsaturated fat, 0 g polyunsaturated fat, 1 g protein, 23 g carbohydrate, 12 mg sodium, 76 mg potassium.

Berry Sauce

0 g fat
0 mg cholesterol

1 **10-ounce package frozen raspberries**
   or **strawberries, thawed**
1 **tablespoon cornstarch**
⅓ **cup red currant jelly**
2 **cups whole raspberries, halved**
   strawberries, *or* sliced peaches

● In a small saucepan combine *undrained* berries and cornstarch. Cook and stir till thickened and bubbly. Cook and stir 2 minutes more. Stir in jelly. Press through a sieve. Discard solids. Cover and chill. Before serving, place berries or peaches in a bowl. Drizzle with sieved mixture. Makes 8 servings.

Nutrition information per serving: 72 calories, 0 g saturated fat, 0 g monounsaturated fat, 0 g polyunsaturated fat, 0 g protein, 19 g carbohydrate, 3 mg sodium, 51 mg potassium.

Fruit Sauce

0 g fat
0 mg cholesterol

1 **8-ounce can pineapple tidbits**
   (juice pack)
⅔ **cup orange juice**
2 **tablespoons sugar**
1 **tablespoon cornstarch**
1 **tablespoon orange liqueur (optional)**
¼ **teaspoon vanilla**
⅛ **teaspoon finely shredded lemon peel**
1 **nectarine, pitted and thinly sliced,**
   or ¾ **cup frozen unsweetened**
   peach slices, thawed
1 **kiwi fruit, peeled, halved lengthwise,**
   and sliced
½ **cup red seedless grapes, halved**

● For sauce, in a small saucepan combine *undrained* pineapple, orange juice, sugar, and cornstarch. Cook and stir till thickened and bubbly. Cook and stir for 2 minutes more. Remove from heat. Stir in liqueur, if desired, and the vanilla and lemon peel. Cover surface with clear plastic wrap and chill.

Before serving, in a bowl combine nectarine or peach slices, kiwi fruit, and grapes. Pour sauce over fruit. Stir gently to coat. Serves 4.

Nutrition information per serving: 123 calories, 0 g saturated fat, 0 g monounsaturated fat, 0 g polyunsaturated fat, 1 g protein, 31 g carbohydrate, 3 mg sodium, 315 mg potassium.

Fruit Fix-Ups

A simple fix-up turns fruit into a special dessert or brunch appetizer without covering up the fresh flavors of the fruit.

● **Oranges Brûlée:** Peel and section 4 *oranges* over an 8x8x2-inch pan or broiler-proof dish to catch juice. Add oranges and one 8¼-ounce can *pineapple chunks,* drained, to the pan. Stir together ¼ cup packed *brown sugar* and ⅛ teaspoon ground *cinnamon;* sprinkle over fruit. Broil 5 inches from heat for 3 to 5 minutes or till sugar bubbles. Garnish with *pineapple leaves* and *raspberries.* Serves 4.

● **Yogurt-Topped Fruit:** In a bowl stir together one 8-ounce carton *orange or lemon low-fat yogurt* and 1 tablespoon *honey.* Stir in 1 to 2 tablespoons *skim milk* to desired consistency. Divide 3 cups *fruit* (halved strawberries, peeled and quartered kiwi fruit, *and/or* seedless grapes) among 4 dessert dishes. Spoon yogurt mixture atop fruit. Serves 4.

● **Sparkling Fruit:** Chill 1½ cups *fruit* (sliced peaches, sliced nectarines, red raspberries, melon balls, *and/or* halved strawberries). *Or,* partially thaw one 10-ounce package frozen light-syrup-pack *mixed fruit or strawberries* (in quick-thaw pouch) according to package directions (about 10 minutes). Divide fruit among 3 dessert dishes. Sprinkle ¼ teaspoon *lemon juice or* 1 teaspoon *amaretto* over *each* dish of fruit. Add 2 tablespoons chilled *ginger ale* to *each* dish. Garnish with mint sprigs, if desired. Serve immediately. Serves 3.

Understanding Fat and Cholesterol

Everywhere you turn these days, someone tells you to cut your fat and cholesterol intake. Do you know why? On the next few pages, you'll find answers to this and other common questions about fat and cholesterol.

Fat and Cholesterol

To help you understand how our bodies digest fat and cholesterol, start by referring to the tip on page 116 for some definitions. Then, check out these questions and answers.

Talking Fat

Why might too much fat in my diet be bad for my health?

A diet high in fat appears to increase the risk of heart disease, the number one cause of death in the United States. A high-fat diet also may increase the risk of diabetes, hypertension, and certain kinds of cancers.

In addition, fat is very high in calories. Reducing fat in your diet can help you to lose weight or to maintain your present weight because you'll likely consume fewer calories, too.

How is the fat in my food related to heart disease?

A high intake of saturated fat can lead to increased blood cholesterol levels. In the past few years, substantial evidence has accumulated showing that as blood cholesterol levels increase so does the risk of heart disease. In most people, a decrease in saturated fat in the diet decreases cholesterol levels in the blood, which probably decreases the risk of heart disease.

What evidence supports this relationship?

The evidence is quite substantial. One ongoing study traces the health of the population of Framingham, Massachusetts, over the past 40 years. The data show that the risk of a heart attack in individuals increases as blood cholesterol level increases.

Studies of populations in different countries also link high-fat diets to an increased risk of heart disease. Japan and Finland are two extremes. In Japan, most people consume a diet low in saturated fat, and the nation has a significantly lower incidence of heart disease than in Finland, where the average diet contains a large amount of saturated fat.

Is the American diet high in fat?

The average American consumes 37 percent of his or her calories as fat. The U.S. Surgeon General, American Heart Association, and other public health organizations feel that this is too high. They recommend that all Americans reduce their fat intake to no more than 30 percent of their total calories. For some people, cutting fat calories to 30 percent will require only slight changes. Others will need to make a drastic reduction to meet these guidelines.

Your Body and Fat and Cholesterol

How much fat do I need in my diet?

Only 1 or 2 tablespoons a day. Since fat occurs in many foods, this amount is easily reached. You need fat to carry fat-soluble vitamins through the body and to provide linoleic acid, a fatty acid essential to good health.

How many calories does fat provide?

One gram of fat contains nine calories, whereas 1 gram of either carbohydrate or protein contains four calories. So, by weight fat has more than twice as many calories as carbohydrate or protein. You can see that fat calories can add up pretty fast.

How can too much fat and cholesterol affect my arteries?

Some of the fat and cholesterol, circulating in your blood is deposited on the inner artery walls. The cholesterol combines with fats and other materials to form hard deposits called plaque. As plaque builds, the artery narrows, reducing the flow of blood. This condition, called atherosclerosis, can lead to a heart attack or a stroke.

115

Fat and Cholesterol Definitions

Saturated Fats: All fats are made of carbon and hydrogen atoms. The carbon atoms form a chain and the hydrogen atoms attach to the chain. When hydrogen atoms are linked to every possible spot on the carbon chain, the fat is called saturated. Most saturated fats are solid at room temperature. Saturated fats occur primarily in meat and dairy products. They also are found in palm oil, palm kernel oil, coconut oil, and coconuts, which are used in many snacks, crackers, and sweets.

Unsaturated Fats: In unsaturated fats, the carbon chain is not completely filled with hydrogen atoms. Monounsaturated fats have one opening and polyunsaturated fats have two or more openings. These fats are liquid or soft at room temperature.

Triglycerides: The term triglycerides is just another name for the fats in our foods and in our bodies. They may be saturated or unsaturated. In our bodies, they occcur as body fat and in the bloodstream. In some individuals they become too high in the blood, and may warrant monitoring.

Cholesterol: Cholesterol is a waxy, fatlike substance that helps form cell membranes, builds nerve sheaths, and serves as the raw material for hormones. Our bodies produce cholesterol (blood cholesterol), but we also ingest cholesterol (dietary cholesterol) when we eat foods of animal origin. Cholesterol travels through the blood attached to a protein. These cholesterol-protein packages are called lipoproteins.

HDL Cholesterol: HDL stands for high density lipoprotein. This type of cholesterol is headed back to the liver to be processed and excreted. Sometimes you hear this referred to as good cholesterol. Exercise and a diet low in saturated fat may raise HDL levels.

LDL Cholesterol: LDL refers to low density lipoprotein cholesterol. This type makes up most of the cholesterol in the body. The low density lipoproteins carry the cholesterol to the cells. When there's more cholesterol than the body needs, the low density lipoproteins deposit cholesterol on artery walls. This build up contributes to atherosclerosis. That's why LDL cholesterol often is called bad cholesterol. A diet low in saturated fats can lower LDL levels.

What effect does the cholesterol in the food I eat have on the cholesterol level in my blood?
The relationship between cholesterol in foods and blood cholesterol levels is not well understood. Consuming too much saturated fat appears to be the key dietary factor in high blood cholesterol. Dietary cholesterol appears to have a lesser effect on blood cholesterol. So, it's still important to limit cholesterol in your diet, especially if your blood cholesterol count is over 200. Most public health organizations recommend that you eat no more than 300 milligrams of cholesterol per day.

Will a low-fat, low-cholesterol diet guarantee lower cholesterol levels in my blood?
Diet is a major factor in blood cholesterol levels, but not the only one. Some people can eat almost anything and maintain a normal healthful cholesterol level, while others follow a low-fat diet and have difficulty reducing their cholesterol to an acceptable level. Most people can, however, lower blood cholesterol levels by reducing saturated fat and cholesterol in their diet. Apparently, each of our bodies handles cholesterol differently. Some people seem to inherit a genetic tendency toward high cholesterol. If your family has a history of high cholesterol or heart disease, take steps now to monitor your cholesterol level.

Also, men tend to have higher cholesterol levels than premenopausal women of the same age. And, for both men and women, cholesterol levels increase with age.

Checking Your Cholesterol Level

I don't know my cholesterol level. Should I have it checked?
If you're an adult over the age of 20, you should know your current cholesterol level and have it checked at least every five years. Since you can count on your cholesterol level rising as you grow older, you'll be able to monitor increases, and, if necessary, take action before you reach the high-risk category.

Where should I go to have my blood cholesterol checked?
You can ask your doctor to check it, or take advantage of one of the screening programs in the shopping malls. Often, a drop of blood obtained by pricking your finger provides enough blood for the test.

What test should I have?
Start with a total blood cholesterol test. This is the type of test offered in shopping malls. It is inexpensive, easy to do, and almost painless. If your total blood cholesterol level is less than 200 mg/dl, most likely you don't have much to worry about.

However, if your cholesterol is near or more than 200 mg/dl, have your doctor do a second test to double check the initial findings. And, consult your doctor for a lipoprotein analysis.

What does a lipoprotein analysis tell me?
This test separately reports your HDL-cholesterol, LDL-cholesterol, triglycerides, and total cholesterol level. It's more expensive than the total blood cholesterol test, and you must fast for 12 hours before the blood is drawn for the analysis.

What if my cholesterol level checks out okay?
It's still a good idea to watch how much fat and cholesterol you eat for the rest of your life. And, have your total cholesterol checked at least every five years.

What if my cholesterol level is too high?
If you have high blood cholesterol, your doctor probably will recommend that you try to lower it through diet. You should have your cholesterol level checked four to six weeks after you begin your diet and again after three months. If you haven't reached your cholesterol goal in three months, your doctor may prescribe further measures.

Once you reach your cholesterol goal, keep to your diet. Have a lipoprotein analysis once a year, and a total cholesterol test at midyear.

What if my triglyceride level is too high?
Some evidence suggests that high blood triglycerides may be a factor in heart disease, but the relationship is not well understood.

What measures will lower my triglycerides?
The diet for lowering triglycerides is basically a low-fat diet. But, in addition to reducing saturated fat and total fat, cut back on sugar and alcohol, too.

How High Is High?

When you are talking about a total cholesterol reading from a blood test, high means more than 240 mg/dl (milligrams of cholesterol per deciliter of blood). A "high" reading indicates an increased risk for heart disease. If your cholesterol level falls between 200 and 239 mg/dl you're classified as "borderline-high." Desirable total cholesterol is less than 200 mg/dl.

If your total cholesterol level is more than 200, your doctor will look at your LDL and HDL cholesterol levels. For LDL cholesterol, a reading of more than 160 mg/dl is considered high risk. A reading from 130 to 159 mg/dl is borderline-high and a desirable level is less than 130 mg/dl.

HDL cholesterol is the only reading where higher is better. A good HDL level is greater than 35 ml/dl. Anything less than this is too low.

Your doctor also may talk about your triglyceride level. A desirable triglyceride level falls between 40 to 150 mg/dl. Anything more is too high.

Dietary Steps to Lower Cholesterol

If you have high blood cholesterol, follow your doctor's advice. The recommendations are likely to include modifications in your diet. And, that's where we can help. Here are answers to some of the questions you may have.

What changes do I need to make in my diet to lower my blood cholesterol?
Follow the recommendations given in the tip on page 5. In addition, aim for 50 to 60 percent of your calories to come from carbohydrates such as cereals, breads, pasta, vegetables, and fruits. And, adjust your caloric intake to just what's needed to achieve or maintain your desirable weight.

How can I raise my HDL level?
Although some foods appear to raise HDL cholesterol, your best bet is a program of regular moderate exercise. A daily brisk 20- to 30-minute walk appears to do the trick. Smoking reduces HDL cholesterol, so if you smoke, stop. And, as your weight increases, HDL levels decline. So, if you're overweight, try to lose excess pounds.

Why do I hear more about reducing saturated fat than other fats?
Saturated fat in the diet has been shown to increase blood cholesterol more than anything else people eat. So, saturated fat is definitely more of a concern than unsaturated fat, especially if you're at risk for

heart disease. Ideally, you should consume about the same amount of each type of fat. (See tip, page 5.)

Why do I need to watch the amount of polyunsaturated fat and monounsaturated fat in my diet?
Evidence suggests that poly unsaturated and monounsaturated fats can lower blood cholesterol. However, these fats contain as many calories as saturated fat so it's a good idea to cut down on total fat.

Will eating oat bran solve my cholesterol woes?
Some evidence indicates that it might. Eating oat bran and other soluble fibers has helped some people lower their blood cholesterol levels. Many foods besides oat bran—dried beans, carrots, corn, and apples, for example—contain soluble fiber.

Remember though, increasing soluble fiber is not a substitute for decreasing fat in your diet. Reducing saturated fat is the single most important step to lower blood cholesterol levels.

How much soluble fiber do I need to eat to lower my blood cholesterol?
Currently, there are no federal dietary recommendations for the amount of soluble fiber we need. A good rule of thumb is 6 grams of soluble fiber for every 1,000 calories that you eat, up to 18 grams. Since most foods list only total fiber content, not soluble fiber, it can be quite difficult to compute your fiber intake. To assure that you receive adequate fiber, eat plenty of whole grains, vegetables, and fruits.

If I follow the prescribed dietary guidelines, how soon will I notice a change in my cholesterol level?
You can expect results in six weeks to six months. Over time you may reduce cholesterol by 30 to 55 mg/dl or more. The more you reduce your cholesterol level, the more you reduce your risk of heart disease.

My cholesterol level is fine. Do I still need to watch fat?
It's still wise to limit fat calories to no more than 30 percent of your total calories. Diets high in fat have been linked to certain cancers, particularly those of the breast, colon, lining of the uterus, and prostate gland.

Also, since most people's cholesterol levels tend to rise with age, reducing fat in your diet *now* may lower your risk of heart disease later in life.

Should I worry about fat and cholesterol in my child's diet?
Children under the age of two need adequate levels of fat to meet calorie needs and to grown and develop normally. Do not restrict fat and cholesterol in the diet of any child under the age of two.

Unfortunately, some older children are showing higher than normal cholesterol levels. Therefore, children should avoid too much fat and cholesterol. Health professionals don't agree yet on the acceptable fat intake for children over two. Some recommend 30 percent calories from fat. Others take a more moderate approach and recommend 30 to 40 percent calories from fat, to allow for growth and development.

Fat and Cholesterol Chart

Keep track of the fat and cholesterol in the foods you eat with this handy chart.

FOOD ITEMS	Fat (g)	Chol. (mg)
ALFALFA SPROUTS; 1 cup	0	0
APPLE BUTTER; 1 tablespoon	1	0
APPLES; 1 medium	1	0
APPLESAUCE, canned; 1 cup	0	0
APRICOTS Canned; 3 halves	0	0
Dried, uncooked; 1 cup	1	0
Fresh; 1 medium	0	0
ARTICHOKES, cooked; 1	0	0
ASPARAGUS, cooked; 4 medium spears	0	0
AVOCADOS; ½ avocado	15	0
BAKING POWDER; 1 teaspoon	0	0
BAKING SODA; 1 teaspoon	0	0
BANANAS; 1 medium	0	0
BARBECUE SAUCE, bottled; ¼ cup	4	0
BARLEY, PEARL, uncooked; 1 cup	2	0
BEANS Baked, with tomato sauce and pork, canned; ½ cup	3	5
Garbanzo, cooked; 1 cup	6	0
Green snap, cooked; ½ cup	0	0
Kidney, red, canned; 1 cup	1	0
Lima, cooked; 1 cup	1	0
Refried, canned; ½ cup	2	0
BEAN SPROUTS, fresh; ½ cup	0	0
BEEF Beef for stew, lean only, cooked cubes; ½ cup	7	102
Corned, cooked, lean only; 3 ounces	26	80
Dried, chipped; 2.5 ounces	4	46
Flank steak, cooked, lean only; 3 ounces	6	80
Ground beef, cooked, 10% fat; 3 ounces	10	80

FOOD ITEMS	Fat (g)	Chol. (mg)
BEEF (continued) Ground beef, cooked, 21% fat; 3 ounces	17	80
Liver, fried; 3 ounces	9	372
Rib roast, cooked, lean only; 3 ounces	11	77
Round steak, cooked, lean only; 3 ounces	5	77
Rump roast, cooked, lean only; 3 ounces	8	78
Short ribs, cooked, lean only; 2½ ounces	24	51
Sirloin steak, cooked, lean only; 3 ounces	6	77
T-bone steak, cooked, lean only; 3 ounces	9	78
Tenderloin, cooked, lean only; 3 ounces	8	47
BEETS, cooked, sliced; ½ cup	0	0
BEVERAGES, alcoholic Beer; 12 ounces	0	0
Dessert wine; 1 ounce	0	0
Gin, rum, vodka, or whiskey; 1 ounce	0	0
Table wine; 1 ounce	0	0
BEVERAGES, nonalcoholic Club soda; 8 ounces	0	0
Cocoa mix; 1 teaspoon	1	2
Coffee, cola, or tea; 8 ounces	0	0
BISCUITS From mix; 1	3	0
From refrigerator dough; 1	2	1
BLACKBERRIES, fresh or frozen; ½ cup	1	0
BLACK-EYED PEAS, cooked; 1 cup	1	0
BLUEBERRIES, fresh or frozen; ½ cup	0	0
BOUILLON, instant granules; 1 teaspoon	0	2
BREAD (see also Rolls) Bagel, plain; 1	2	0
Corn bread; 1 piece (2½x2½x1½ inches)	5	61
Croissant; 1	12	13
Crumbs, dry; ¼ cup	1	1

FOOD ITEMS	Fat (g)	Chol. (mg)
BREAD (continued) Crumbs, soft; ¼ cup	0	0
French; 1 slice (2½x2½x½ inches)	0	0
Pita; 1 pocket	0	0
Pumpernickel; 1 slice	1	0
Raisin; 1 slice	1	1
Rye; 1 slice	1	0
White; 1 slice	1	1
Whole wheat; 1 slice	1	1
BROCCOLI, cooked; 2 medium spears	0	0
BROWNIES; 1 (1¾-inch square)	6	18
BRUSSELS SPROUTS, cooked; ½ cup	0	0
BULGUR, uncooked; 1 cup	3	0
BUTTER, regular; 1 tablespoon	12	36
CABBAGE, raw, shredded; 1 cup	0	0
CAKES, baked from home recipes Angel, no icing; $1/12$ cake	0	0
Carrot, cream cheese frosting, 10-inch ring; $1/16$ cake	21	74
Chocolate, 2 layers, chocolate icing; $1/12$ cake	13	37
Pound, loaf; $1/17$ cake	5	32
Sponge, no icing; $1/12$ cake	4	155
White, uncooked white icing; $1/12$ cake	13	8
Yellow, chocolate icing; $1/12$ cake	13	42
CANDY Caramels; 1 ounce (3 medium)	3	1
Chocolate bar, milk, plain; 1 ounce	9	6
Chocolate bar, milk, with almonds; 1 ounce	10	5
Chocolate fudge; 1 piece (1 ounce)	5	1
Gumdrops; 1 ounce	0	0
Peanut brittle; 1 ounce	3	0
CANTALOUPE; ¼ medium	0	0
CARROTS, raw; 1 medium	0	0
CATSUP; 1 tablespoon	0	0
CAULIFLOWER, cooked; ½ cup	0	0
CELERY, raw; 1 stalk	0	0
CELERY SEED; 1 teaspoon	1	0
CEREALS, cooked Oat bran; ⅓ cup	2	0
Oatmeal; ½ cup	1	0
Wheat, rolled; ½ cup	0	0

FOOD ITEMS	Fat (g)	Chol. (mg)
CEREALS, ready-to-eat Bite-size shredded wheat biscuits; ½ cup	0	0
Bran flakes; ½ cup	0	0
Cornflakes; ½ cup	0	0
Granola; ¼ cup	4	0
Rice, crisp cereal; ½ cup	0	0
Wheat flakes; ½ cup	0	0
CHEESE American; 1 ounce	9	26
Blue; 1 ounce	9	25
Brie; 1 ounce	8	28
Cheddar; 1 ounce	9	28
Cottage, cream-style; ½ cup	5	22
Cottage, dry; ½ cup	0	5
Cottage, low-fat; ½ cup	2	10
Cream cheese; 1 ounce	11	31
Cream cheese, reduced-calorie; 1 ounce	5	15
Feta; 1 ounce	6	25
Monterey Jack; 1 ounce	9	28
Mozzarella, part skim milk; 1 ounce	5	15
Mozzarella, whole milk; 1 ounce	6	22
Muenster; 1 ounce	9	27
Neufchâtel; 1 ounce	7	22
Parmesan, grated; 1 tablespoon	1	5
Provolone; 1 ounce	8	20
Ricotta, part skim milk; ½ cup	10	38
Ricotta, whole milk; ½ cup	16	62
Spread, American; 1 ounce	6	18
Swiss, natural; 1 ounce	8	28
Swiss, process; 1 ounce	7	24
CHEESECAKE, 9-inch; $1/12$ cake	18	170
CHERRIES; 10	0	0
CHICKEN Broiler, broiled with skin; 4 ounces	10	67
Dark meat, skinned, roasted; 4 ounces	6	56
Fryer, batter-fried with skin; 4 ounces	15	77
Light meat, skinned, roasted; 4 ounces	3	56
Roaster, roasted with skin; 4 ounces	9	70

FOOD ITEMS	Fat (g)	Chol. (mg)
CHICKEN LIVERS, cooked, chopped; 1 cup	8	883
CHILI POWDER; 1 teaspoon	0	0
CHOCOLATE Semisweet; 1 ounce	10	0
Syrup, fudge-type; 1 tablespoon	3	0
Syrup, thin-type; 1 tablespoon	0	0
Unsweetened; 1 ounce	15	0
CINNAMON, ground; 1 teaspoon	0	0
CLAMS, raw Hard; 3 ounces	1	43
Soft; 3 ounces	2	43
COCOA POWDER, unsweetened; 1 tablespoon	1	0
COCONUT, dried, sweetened, shredded; ½ cup	16	0
COFFEE CAKE, crumb, from mix; ⅙ cake	7	47
COOKIES Chocolate chip; 1 (2¼-inch diameter)	2	4
Cream sandwich, chocolate; 1	2	4
Fig bar; 1 (1⅝-inch square)	1	7
Oatmeal, with raisins; 1 (2⅝-inch diameter)	3	1
Peanut butter; 1 (2⅝-inch diameter)	4	6
Sugar; 1 (2¼-inch diameter)	1	3
Vanilla wafer; 1 (1⅜-inch diameter)	0	1
COOKING OIL; 1 tablespoon	14	0
CORN Canned, cream-style; ½ cup	1	0
Cooked; ½ cup	0	0
CORN CHIPS; 1 ounce	10	9
CORNMEAL; 1 cup	2	0
CORNSTARCH; 1 tablespoon	0	0
CORN SYRUP; 1 tablespoon	0	0
CRABMEAT, cooked; 3 ounces	2	86
CRACKERS Butter, rectangular; 1	1	0
Cheese, round; 1	1	1
Graham; 2 squares	1	0
Rye wafer, crisp; 2 (3½x1⅞ inches)	0	0
Saltine; 2 (2-inch squares)	1	0
CRANBERRIES Cranberry juice cocktail; 1 cup	0	0
Cranberry sauce; ½ cup	0	0

FOOD ITEMS	Fat (g)	Chol. (mg)
CREAM Half and half; 1 tablespoon	2	6
Light; 1 tablespoon	5	17
Whipping; 1 tablespoon	6	20
CUCUMBERS; 6 large slices (1 ounce)	0	0
DANISH PASTRY, fruit; 1	13	56
DATES, fresh or dried, pitted; 10	0	0
DOUGHNUTS Cake-type, plain; 1 medium	8	25
Yeast-type; 1 medium	11	11
DUCK, roasted, flesh only; ½ duck	25	197
EGGS White; 1 large	0	0
Whole; 1 large	6	210
Yolk; 1 large	5	210
EGGNOG; 1 cup	19	149
EGGPLANT, cooked, chopped; ½ cup	0	0
EGG SUBSTITUTE, liquid; 1 cup	8	3
ENGLISH MUFFIN, plain; 1	1	0
FAST FOOD ENTRÉES Cheeseburger, regular; 1	15	44
Cheeseburger, ¼-pound patty; 1	31	104
Fish sandwich with cheese; 1	23	56
Hamburger, regular; 1	11	32
Hamburger, ¼-pound patty; 1	21	71
Roast beef sandwich; 1	13	55
Taco; 1	11	21
FIGS, dried; 10	2	0
FISH Cod, broiled with butter; 3 ounces	5	69
Fish sticks, frozen, reheated; 1 fish stick	3	26
Flounder or sole, baked with butter; 3 ounces	6	68
Flounder or sole, baked without added fat; 3 ounces	1	59
Haddock, broiled; 2.5 ounces	0	55
Halibut, broiled with butter; 3 ounces	6	62
Salmon, broiled with butter; 3 ounces	6	39
Salmon, canned, pink; 3 ounces	5	30
Sardines, canned, in oil, drained; 3 ounces	9	120
Snapper, broiled; 2.5 ounces	1	55
Trout, broiled with butter; 3 ounces	9	71
Tuna, canned, in oil; 3 ounces	18	47

FOOD ITEMS	Fat (g)	Chol. (mg)
FISH (continued) Tuna, canned, in water; 3 ounces	1	54
Walleye pike, broiled; 2.5 ounces	1	48
FLOUR, wheat All-purpose; 1 cup	1	0
Whole wheat; 1 cup	2	0
FRANKFURTER, cooked; 1 medium	12	27
FRENCH TOAST; 1 slice	7	112
FRUIT PUNCH DRINK; 6 ounces	0	0
GARLIC; 1 clove	0	0
GELATIN, dry, unflavored; 1 envelope	0	0
GINGERBREAD, square; $1/9$ cake	4	1
GOOSE, cooked; 3 ounces	30	73
GRAPEFRUIT; $1/2$ medium	0	0
GRAPES, green, seedless; $1/2$ cup	0	0
GRAVIES Beef, canned; 1 cup	5	7
Brown, from dry mix; 1 cup	2	2
Chicken, canned; 1 cup	14	5
Chicken, from dry mix; 1 cup	2	3
Mushroom, canned; 1 cup	6	0
HONEY; 1 tablespoon	0	0
HONEYDEW MELON; $1/4$ medium	1	0
ICE CREAM, vanilla Regular; 1 cup	14	53
Soft-serve; 1 cup	14	53
ICE MILK, vanilla; $1/2$ cup	6	18
KIWI FRUIT; 1	0	0
LAMB Leg roast, cooked, lean only; 3 ounces	6	85
Loin chop, cooked, lean only; 3 ounces	6	84
Rib chop, cooked, lean only; 3 ounces	9	86
LARD; 1 tablespoon	13	12
LEMON JUICE; 1 tablespoon	0	0
LEMONADE; 6 ounces	0	0
LENTILS, cooked; $1/2$ cup	0	0
LETTUCE, iceberg; $1/4$ medium head	0	0
LOBSTER, cooked; $1/2$ cup	1	62
LUNCHEON MEATS Bologna; 2 ounces	16	31
Braunschweiger; 2 ounces	18	89
Salami; 2 ounces	11	37

FOOD ITEMS	Fat (g)	Chol. (mg)
MACARONI, cooked; $1/2$ cup	0	0
MARGARINE Regular; 1 tablespoon	12	0
Spread, low-calorie; 1 tablespoon	5	0
MARSHMALLOWS; 1 ounce	0	0
MELBA TOAST, plain; 1 piece	0	0
MILK Buttermilk; 1 cup	0	5
Dried nonfat, instant, reconstituted; 1 cup	1	15
Evaporated, skim, undiluted; 1 cup	1	8
Evaporated, undiluted; 1 cup	20	78
Low-fat (2%); 1 cup	5	22
Skim; 1 cup	0	5
Sweetened, condensed, undiluted; 1 cup	27	104
Whole; 1 cup	9	34
MILK SHAKES Chocolate; 10 ounces	8	30
Vanilla; 10 ounces	9	33
MOLASSES; 1 tablespoon	0	0
MUFFINS, baked from home recipes Blueberry; 1	4	33
Bran; 1	4	41
Corn; 1	5	23
Plain; 1	4	21
MUSHROOMS, fresh, sliced; 1 cup	0	0
MUSTARD, prepared; 1 teaspoon	0	0
NECTARINES; 1 medium	0	0
NONDAIRY TOPPING Frozen; 1 tablespoon	1	0
Powdered; 1 teaspoon	1	0
NOODLES Chow mein, canned; 1 cup	11	5
Egg, cooked; $1/2$ cup	1	25
NUTS Almonds, roasted; 1 ounce (about 22)	16	0
Cashews, roasted; $1/4$ cup	16	0
Filberts (hazelnuts), chopped; $1/4$ cup	18	0
Peanuts, roasted; $1/4$ cup	18	0
Pecans, chopped; $1/4$ cup	21	0
Pistachio nuts, dried; 1 ounce	14	0
Walnuts, chopped; $1/4$ cup	19	0

FOOD ITEMS	Fat (g)	Chol. (mg)
OLIVES Green; 4 medium	2	0
Ripe; 4 medium	3	0
OKRA, cooked; 8 pods	0	0
ONIONS Cooked, sliced; ½ cup	0	0
French-fried rings; 1 ounce	15	0
ORANGE JUICE; 1 cup	0	0
ORANGES; 1 medium	0	0
OYSTERS, raw; ½ cup (6 to 10 medium)	8	170
PANCAKES, made from mix; 1 (4-inch)	2	20
PAPAYA; 1 medium	0	0
PARSLEY; 10 sprigs	0	0
PEACHES 1 medium	0	0
Canned; ½ peach	0	0
PEANUT BUTTER; 1 tablespoon	8	0
PEARS 1 medium	1	0
Canned; ½ pear	0	0
PEAS, cooked; ½ cup	0	0
PEPPERS, green, sweet, chopped; ½ cup	0	0
PICKLES Dill; 1 large (4x1¾ inches)	0	0
Sweet; 1 medium (2¾x¾ inches)	0	0
PIE; ⅛ of a 9-inch pie Apple, blueberry, cherry, or peach	14	0
Custard	13	126
Lemon meringue	11	107
Pecan	24	71
Pumpkin	13	82
PIE SHELL, baked; one 9-inch	60	0
PINEAPPLE, canned; 1 slice	0	0
PINEAPPLE JUICE, unsweetened; 1 cup	0	0
PIZZA, cheese, 15-inch; ⅛ pizza	9	56
PLUMS, fresh; 1 (2-inch diameter)	0	0
POPCORN, plain, popped; 1 cup	0	0
PORK, cooked Bacon, Canadian-style; 2 slices	4	27
Bacon, strips, medium thickness; 3	9	16
Chop, loin center cut, lean only; 3 ounces	13	74

FOOD ITEMS	Fat (g)	Chol. (mg)
PORK (continued) Ham, fully cooked, lean only; 3 ounces	19	77
Picnic shoulder, lean only; 2.4 ounces	8	76
Ribs, lean only; 2.5 ounces	10	56
POTATO CHIPS; 10 medium	8	0
POTATOES Au gratin, from dry mix; 1 cup	10	12
Baked; 1 medium	0	0
French-fried, frozen, oven heated; 10 medium	4	0
Hash browns, from frozen; 1 cup	5	12
Mashed, with milk and margarine; 1 cup	9	4
Scalloped, from dry mix; 1 cup	11	27
PRETZELS; 10 small sticks	0	0
PRUNES, dried, uncooked, pitted; ½ cup	0	0
PUDDING, prepared from dry mix with whole milk Chocolate; ½ cup	4	15
Rice; ½ cup	4	15
Tapioca; ½ cup	4	15
Vanilla; ½ cup	4	15
PUMPKIN, canned; 1 cup	1	0
RADISHES, raw; 5 medium	0	0
RAISINS; 1 cup	0	0
RASPBERRIES, fresh; ½ cup	1	0
RHUBARB, cooked, sweetened; ½ cup	0	0
RICE Brown, cooked; ½ cup	1	0
Quick cooking; ½ cup	0	0
White, cooked; ½ cup	0	0
ROLLS Dinner; 1	2	0
Hamburger or frankfurter bun; 1	2	2
Hard; 1 medium	1	1
Sweet; 1 medium	10	27
SALAD DRESSINGS Blue cheese, reduced-calorie; 1 tablespoon	1	0
Blue cheese, regular; 1 tablespoon	8	3
French, reduced-calorie; 1 tablespoon	1	0
French, regular; 1 tablespoon	6	0
Italian, reduced-calorie; 1 tablespoon	1	0

FOOD ITEMS	Fat (g)	Chol. (mg)
SALAD DRESSINGS (continued) Italian, regular; 1 tablespoon	9	0
Mayonnaise; 1 tablespoon	11	10
Mayonnaise-type, reduced-calorie; 1 tablespoon	2	8
Mayonnaise-type, regular; 1 tablespoon	6	8
Thousand Island, reduced-calorie; 1 tablespoon	2	8
Thousand Island, regular; 1 tablespoon	8	8
SAUERKRAUT, canned; ½ cup	0	0
SAUSAGES Brown and serve sausage (10 per package), cooked; 1 link	5	9
Italian sausage, cooked; 1 ounce	7	21
Pepperoni; 1 ounce	12	17
Pork sausage, cooked; 1 link	6	12
SCALLOPS, cooked; 3 ounces	1	46
SHERBET, orange; ½ cup	1	0
SHORTENING; 1 tablespoon	13	0
SHRIMP Canned; 3 ounces	1	129
French-fried; 3 ounces	9	129
Raw; 3 ounces	1	135
SOUPS, condensed, canned, diluted with water unless specified otherwise Beef bouillon, broth, or consommé; 1 cup	0	0
Beef noodle; 1 cup	3	17
Chicken broth; 1 cup	0	0
Chicken noodle; 1 cup	2	14
Clam chowder, Manhattan-style; 1 cup	2	10
Cream of celery, diluted with milk; 1 cup	9	25
Cream of mushroom, diluted with milk; 1 cup	14	27
Split pea soup; 1 cup	3	5
Tomato; 1 cup	2	0
Tomato, diluted with milk; 1 cup	7	18
Vegetable with beef broth; 1 cup	2	10
SOUR CREAM, dairy; 1 cup	48	102
SOY SAUCE; 1 teaspoon	0	0
SPAGHETTI, cooked; ½ cup	0	0
SPINACH, fresh, torn; 1 cup	0	0

FOOD ITEMS	Fat (g)	Chol. (mg)
SQUASH Summer, cooked, chopped; ½ cup	0	0
Winter, baked, mashed; ½ cup	0	0
STRAWBERRIES, fresh, whole; 1 cup	1	0
SUGAR Brown; 1 tablespoon	0	0
Granulated; 1 tablespoon	0	0
SUNFLOWER SEEDS; 1 ounce	14	0
SWEET POTATOES, boiled; 1 potato	0	0
TANGARINE; 1	0	0
TARTAR SAUCE; 1 tablespoon	8	0
TOFU (soybean curd); 4 ounces	5	0
TOMATOES Fresh; 1 medium	0	0
Canned; 1 cup	1	0
Paste, canned; 6 ounces	1	0
Sauce, canned; 8 ounces	0	0
TORTILLAS Corn; 1 (6-inch)	1	0
Flour; 1 (6-inch)	2	0
TURKEY Dark meat, roasted, flesh only; 3 ounces	6	72
Ham, cured; 2 ounces	3	32
Light meat, roasted, flesh only; 3 ounces	3	59
Patty, breaded; 1 (2.25 ounces)	12	40
VEAL Cutlet, cooked; 3 ounces	11	86
Loin chop, cooked; 3 ounces	12	76
VEGETABLE JUICE COCKTAIL; 1 cup	0	0
WAFFLES; 1 section (4½x4½x⅝ inches)	5	63
WATER CHESTNUTS, canned and drained; 1 cup	0	0
WATERMELON; 1 wedge (8x4 inches)	1	0
WHIPPED TOPPING, mix; 1 envelope	13	0
WHITE SAUCE From dry mix; 1 cup	13	34
From home recipe; 1 cup	30	32
YOGURT Fruit-flavored; ½ cup	1	5
Non-fat; ½ cup	0	2
Plain; ½ cup	2	7

Index

BETTER HOMES AND GARDENS® BOOKS
Editor: Gerald M. Knox
Art Director: Ernest Shelton
Managing Editor: David A. Kirchner
Project Editors: James D. Blume, Marsha Jahns
Editorial Project Managers: Liz Anderson, Jennifer Speer Ramundt, Angela K. Renkoski

Department Head, Food and Family Life Books: Sharyl Heiken
Associate Department Heads: Sandra Granseth, Rosemary C. Hutchinson, Elizabeth Woolever
Senior Food Editors: Linda Henry, Mary Jo Plutt, Joyce Trollope
Associate Food Editors: Jennifer Darling, Debra-Ann Duggan, Heather M. Hephner, Mary Major, Shelli McConnell
Test Kitchen: Director, Sharon Stilwell; Photo Studio Director, Janet Herwig
Home Economists: Lynn Blanchard, Kay Cargill, Marilyn Cornelius, Maryellyn Krantz, Marge Steenson, Colleen Weeden

Associate Art Directors: Neoma Thomas, Linda Ford Vermie, Randall Yontz
Assistant Art Directors: Lynda Haupert, Harijs Priekulis, Tom Wegner
Graphic Designers: Mary Schlueter Bendgen, Michael Burns, Brenda Drake Lesch
Art Production: Director, John Berg; Associate, Joe Heuer; Office Manager, Michaela Lester

President, Book Group: Jeramy Lanigan
Vice President, Retail Marketing: Jamie Martin
Vice President, Administrative Services: Rick Rundall

BETTER HOMES AND GARDENS® MAGAZINE
President, Magazine Group: James A. Autry
Vice President, Editorial Director: Doris Eby
Food and Nutrition Editor: Nancy Byal

MEREDITH CORPORATE OFFICERS
Chairman of the Executive Committee: E. T. Meredith III
Chairman of the Board: Robert A. Burnett
President: Jack D. Rehm

LOW-FAT MEALS
Editor: Mary Major
Editorial Project Manager: Jennifer Speer Ramundt
Graphic Designer: Mary Schlueter Bendgen
Electronic Text Processor: Paula Forest
Contributing Editor: Sandra Mosley
Contributing Food Stylist: Joanne Cherry, Suzanne Finley
Contributing Photographers: Dennis Becker, Sean Fitzgerald, Michael Jensen

Have BETTER HOMES AND GARDENS® magazine delivered to your door. For information, write to:
MR. ROBERT AUSTIN
P.O. BOX 4536
DES MOINES, IA 50336